PENCILLINGS

Pencillings

by

John Middleton Murry

Essay Index Reprint Series

BOOKS FOR LIBRARIES PRESS
FREEPORT, NEW YORK

First Published 1925
Reprinted 1969

STANDARD BOOK NUMBER:
8369-1229-2

LIBRARY OF CONGRESS CATALOG CARD NUMBER:
70-90666

PRINTED IN THE UNITED STATES OF AMERICA

NOTE

Most of these little essays were published under the title of "Pencillings" in *The Times* during the summer of 1922. A few appeared in the *Nation* and *Athenaeum*. I thank the editors of these newspapers for allowing me to reprint them.

The title "Pencillings" was not my own choice. The title I chose proved too long for the width of a narrow column. To return to it, however, would be misleading.

CONTENTS

	PAGE
CHIAROSCURO	1
THE READER'S DUTY	11
HIGH PLACES	20
DICKENS	31
THE GOLDEN PEN	42
LITERATURE AND SCIENCE	53
A NEW HUMANISM?	62
THE CURÉ OF WANGS	71
THE PROBLEM OF SIZE	81
ON DEPENDABLE WRITERS	90
WHAT IS STYLE?	99
MANNERS AND MORALITY	109
MORALITY AGAIN	119
CLASSICAL TRANSLATIONS	128
DISRAELI ON LOVE	138

CONTENTS

	PAGE
ORATORY AND LITERATURE	147
ON UNPLEASANT CHARACTERS	158
DR. JOHNSON AND THE SWALLOWS	168
SERIOUSNESS	176
THE COURAGE OF CRITICISM	185
ON READING REVIEWS	194
CONGREVE AND MOLIÈRE	203
FACT AND FICTION	213
WHY DO POETS WRITE?	222
STEPHEN PHILLIPS	230
BEAUTY-HUNTING	238
ON GRAMMAR	250
S. P. E.	265

CHIAROSCURO

ONE of the most peculiar features of literature during the last thirty or forty years has been the steady movement of a part of it towards esotericism. To-day literature is divided into the comprehensible and the incomprehensible. The incomprehensible part is naturally not very popular. It is written on the definite assumption that the writer's duty is wholly towards himself, or, as he generally prefers to put it, towards his art. He writes to satisfy a purely personal impulse to self-expression. He writes, just as he chooses the colour of his wall-paper, to please himself alone. He does not hope to be understood, and he

PENCILLINGS

says to himself with a resignation in which there is a tinge of complacency and even of pride, that no really original writer ever has been understood.

Of course this esoteric literature is disregarded by the general public, which even if it desired to regard it, could not do so. The general public has managed, rather dubiously, to swallow Meredith, and is still wondering whether the meal agreed with it; it has made some sort of an effort to cope with Henry James. After that, it has accepted the inevitable and decided that esoteric literature and itself must part. Only just in time. For the difficulty of Henry James is as nothing to the difficulty of some of the literature which has followed him. And yet the general public has managed to take to its heart the greatest

CHIAROSCURO

writer of our time, Thomas Hardy. It has enjoyed Kipling and Wells spontaneously; it has succeeded, with perhaps a little more effort, in acquiring a genuine appetite for Conrad; it has elected Arnold Bennett's finest novel, *The Old Wives' Tale,* into the highest place in its own affections. But we may prophesy with certainty that it will never, never come to terms with the book which is now being announced by initiates as the masterpiece of the age, Mr. James Joyce's *Ulysses.*

It is open to the esoteric to argue that the general public has never really understood Hardy or Conrad or any other great English author. It is probably true in the sense that a very small number of the people who have agonised over the fortunes of Tess or Bathsheba could render a coherent

PENCILLINGS

account of their fascination. But they have loved and re-read the stories, and they remember them. Perhaps there is nobody who understands Hamlet; there are thousands who know him. Don Quixote is vivid in the minds of a hundred times more people than have grasped the definite intention of Cervantes in creating him. And perhaps Don Quixote would be a smaller figure if that intention were generally understood. The mind is more profoundly moved by things it does not wholly understand than by things completely comprehended. A greater magnitude is given to a created character, a deeper significance to a verse of poetry, by the margin of mystery which surrounds it.

But this mystery is not obscurity. When the general public reads a great book it is

CHIAROSCURO

moved by the feeling that the words contain more than they say; but the condition of this feeling is that it should understand what the words actually do say. No one ever failed to follow the story of Don Quixote or Hamlet or to find a simple delight in following it. Dostoevsky's *Crime and Punishment* is one of the most thrilling detective stories in the world, *Madame Bovary* one of the simplest and most absorbing tales of provincial life. And they are that, and they remain that, because they are also something else. They have a source of vitality apart from the interest of their stories. The stories last as stories because they were not told for the story's sake alone. Some passionate conviction about life went to their making, and an ardent desire to express this conviction so clearly, so simply, that no one could refuse to share it. The mystery of a great book lies in its clarity. It is the feeling of wonder that so much should be contained in so little.

At a point of time which many now living are old enough to remember, there sprang into being a heresy which has gained in strength with the years. It began to be believed that the writer had to feel not a passionate conviction about life, but a passionate conviction about art. The heresy came from France. It began to be known in England that two great writers, Flaubert and Baudelaire, had enounced the doctrine of "art for art's sake." (Perhaps it was a misfortune that the word "art" ever came to be mixed up with literature.) It was not known, and it has never been clearly understood to this day, that the passionate

CHIAROSCURO

conviction of those two writers about art was merely a peculiar form imposed by the social conditions of their age upon a passionate conviction about life. They were born at the beginnings of plutocratic industrialism. They believed in art because they passionately disbelieved in life. And the book and poems which they wrote are important precisely in so far as they are directly animated by their deep conviction that life was a torment.

But a tradition was built upon them in the curious persuasion that they were indifferent to life. They were reported to have cultivated art as an end itself, as a transcendental satisfaction beyond the reach of ordinary human beings. They who had spent agonies on trying to be absolutely unmistakable (as they were) were made

PENCILLINGS

the protective deities of literary incomprehensibility. It was a strange aberration in the human mind; and the aberration still flourishes. The conviction that it is superior to be esoteric continues to work havoc among writers of talent and even of genius. The great effort to be unmistakable which distinguishes the man of literary genius from the mere genius (who without it is next door to the madman) is contemptuously called "making concessions."

As if to be unmistakable were necessarily to be popular! As if the effort to be unmistakable were not the very secret of style! As if it were not precisely because the true writer insists that his reader shall feel exactly what he intends him to feel, instead of what the reader would like to feel, that he sometimes has such difficulty

CHIAROSCURO

in getting a hearing! People do not like to be disturbed. Literature exists in order to disturb them. A writer may disturb them by forcing them to think thoughts and feel emotions which they find they really wanted to think and feel. Then, like Dickens, he may be great and popular at once. Another writer may compel them to think and feel things which they do not want to think and feel. He is likely to be a great writer long before he is a popular one, like Thomas Hardy. But if he is unmistakable, his day of popularity will come. It is the unmistakability that matters. In the long run we all accept what we cannot refuse.

Goethe said one day to Eckermann that the writer who did not write in the expectation of a million readers had missed his

PENCILLINGS

vocation. On another day he said also to Eckermann that a writer could not hope to be really understood. The busy commentators have pointed out that there is a contradiction. There is none at all. No one ever understands all that a great writer meant by his creation; perhaps there are few great writers who understand it all themselves. But the writer who flinches in the effort to convey his meaning, or all that he knows of it, in words and characters so clear and compulsive that the last of a million readers must respond is less of a writer than he should be. And that is why a great book, or even a really good book, contains something for every one who will approach it.

THE READER'S DUTY

It is an article of modern literary faith that all great writers were incomprehensible in their day. It is a legend. Comparatively few great writers have not become popular in their lives, and if from them we take away those who died before forty, there are few indeed. What is true is that it often takes a new and original writer longer to reach his public than a facile and familiar one. But not because of his obscurity. It is his clarity which stands in the way. It is a shock for us to be compelled to see life in an unfamiliar light and we fight shy of the experience. But those who risk it return and bring others with them. The

PENCILLINGS

popularity of a great writer may be slow—it is not always—but it is certain. But the writer who elects to be ambiguous remains unpopular for ever.

As soon as a writer ceases to be governed by the desire to enforce his thought and feelings upon us, he becomes something other than a writer, something interesting for the connoisseur of psychology, something far less important for the world at large. When Henry James began to devote his energies to the solution of subtle problems of form which when they were solved could not increase but only weaken the compulsion he exerted on the reader's mind, he was by so much less a writer. He may have been more of an artist. It does not matter if he was. At least it matters only in a private way. It matters only if another

THE READER'S DUTY

writer should arise who, without ever confusing the means with the end, will take advantage of some of Henry James's explorations and use them in order to increase his own unmistakability.

This esoteric significance of certain writers is utterly different from absolute significance. A good teacher in the arts, like a good trainer in boxing, may be an indifferent performer himself. He is so occupied with his method that he forgets his business is to knock out his man. Some writers are always forgetting that. And it is unreasonable for their admirers to denounce the stupidity of a public which does not admire them also. The public expects a writer to be able to knock it out, so soon as it ventures within reach of the blow. That is what it respects him for, and

PENCILLINGS

if he fails in that, he fails in everything. What does the public care, why should it care, if it was he who taught the next champion his punch? That is family history. So it is idle to proclaim that Mallarmé was a great poet. He began by being a true poet and ended by being an incomprehensible one. Other poets may learn from him, and they may be great poets. But that will only be if, unlike him, they do not mistake the means for the end.

What the writer may reasonably ask from the public is more curiosity, more readiness to come within his reach and see whether he can shock them into a new way of looking at life. He has a right to ask that they should approach a new book with the definite expectation of being disturbed, and with the knowledge that the finest pleasure

THE READER'S DUTY

literature has to offer is the revelation which follows upon this shock to fixed habits of thinking and feeling. He has a right to ask that readers should not expect from him a mere reflection of themselves, a gratification of their own daydreams or a titillation of their social curiosities. Of course there are plenty of writers who give these things, and they have their reward. But the persons who ask for them may be excellent members of society; they are not readers. And perhaps they are not even excellent members of society. They are stagnant, they are moribund, they are sliding into spiritual decrepitude.

The writer may fairly demand that they should wake out of it. And we on his behalf may preach the duty of intellectual curiosity. England needs it more than most countries. France is infinitely, Germany much more curious about intellectual things than England. The Americans are passing us by. We are perhaps the nation in the world least eager for new spiritual experiences. A visit to Paris becomes a positive ordeal to one's national self-respect. There are a dozen good bookshops where we find one in London. And the books they contain tell a painful story. An exposition of the Einstein theory by M. Nordmann of the Paris Observatory has passed its fortieth thousand. M. Paul Morand, a young writer whose work would certainly be caviare to the general here, produces a book of brilliant stories, *Ouvert la Nuit*. Seventeen thousand copies have been sold in a fortnight! And, for a final taste of wormwood, imagine the intellectual

THE READER'S DUTY

eagerness of a public which has bought forty thousand copies of each of the five volumes of M. Marcel Proust's remarkable and exacting narrative.

Any one of these happenings would be a portent in England at the present time. If they all happened together we should look for a cataclysm. Of course it may be said that French books are cheaper than English ones. At the present exchange, indeed, they are less than half the price. But though a franc is not a shilling to a Frenchman any more, it is certainly more than sixpence. And there are two great causes why French books are cheaper than English ones. The first is that a French publisher can generally count on three or four times the demand that an English publisher can. The second is that French books are

PENCILLINGS

paper-bound. We are told that paper covers are altogether too flimsy for the solid English taste. No doubt. But the secret of the riddle is that the French public wants the books and not the covers, and that the French library reader has sufficient respect for books to make a paper cover last as long as a cloth case.

The paper-covered book is, in fact, a rough and ready test of literary curiosity. Anglo-Saxondom fails badly by it. So that the moral of this story is double-edged. If the writer has a duty towards the reader, the reader has a duty towards the writer. If the writer shirks or denies his duty, then "the less writer he," though he may be an artist or a genius. If the reader shirks his, he may be a subscriber to four libraries at once, but he is not a reader. The bad

THE READER'S DUTY

reader helps to make the bad writer. Against indifference, indifference sometimes seems the only remedy; and obscurantism the best reply to neglect. But it is not really so. No converts to literature are made by shutting the door of the temple against them. *Compelle intrare* must remain the writer's sign. Compel them to come in —but at the point of the pen.

HIGH PLACES

Most of those who deal much with books have some secret literary dissipation. In a private cupboard they keep a few curious bottles to which they are ever slyly returning. They are willing to admit that these private tipples are not to be compared (in public anyhow) with the established vintages. Yet it is to these they go when all else fails them. They ought to be obeying the sage precept of Matthew Arnold and tuning their palate with the indisputably sublime. But it is not the full flavour they are wanting. It is the tang of personality, almost of eccentricity, they need: a violent stimulant which exactly suits a few mentalities, and may agree with few others.

HIGH PLACES

The most reputable of my own private stimulants form an oddly assorted trio. They are Stendhal's *La Chartreuse de Parme*, Mr. Wells's *The History of Mr. Polly*, and *The Note-Books of Samuel Butler*. Each of these has so far proved infallible when I am suffering from a surfeit of literature. The worst attack of accidie, the veritable devil that walketh in the noonday, gives way before them. Are they all great books? I have often declared that they are, but for the life of me I cannot be sure. Sometimes I doubt whether a great book could be so precisely fitted to my constitution as these are. Indeed, there are moments when my conscience pricks me. I am almost afraid to take them up, without some assurance that my case is really urgent. I may be like a man taking nips from the domestic brandy which is for medicinal purposes only.

Lately, I have been at *La Chartreuse de Parme* again. I do not pretend that *La Chartreuse* is an esoteric devotion of my own. But I fancy its devotees would make a rather strange company. I have pressed it upon many of my friends: I have not yet found one who really took to it. One of them has always maintained that it has no chapter divisions, and when I showed them to him, book in hand, he persisted that they were not in the copy which he tried to read. He also said, I do not know upon what evidence, that Mr. Saintsbury (who is not sympathetic to Stendahl) had remarked upon the same peculiarity. Since the three copies I have possessed—abominably printed, all of them—were " beyond

HIGH PLACES

a peradventure" divided into chapters, I conclude that this is an example of collective hallucination. I myself can never remember the chapters, though I know the book pretty well and adore it; it is perhaps natural that those who do not should be persuaded that it has no chapters at all.

However that may be, I have yet to meet in the flesh a person who knows *La Chartreuse* well enough to discuss its incidents in detail. Undoubtedly they exist, and I sometimes comfort myself with the thought that many of them are very distinguished. Taine read it eighty times; M. André Gide has declared that it is the finest of all French novels; Mr. Maurice Hewlett, I believe, translated it into English; and M. Marcel Proust a year ago made a reference to it

PENCILLINGS

which proved that his knowledge of it was profound, though his memory of the names was at fault. It was M. Proust's reference which gave me the excuse for going back to the book. I wanted to make sure that the Abbé Blanès was not the Abbé Banès as M. Proust called him. He was not. The mistake is a stray evidence of how little Stendhal is read even in his own country. Whether *La Chartreuse* is the finest French novel or not, it is one of the most famous, and the Abbé Blanès is one of the most important characters in it. To call him Banès is not quite as bad as to speak of Mr. Snowgrass; but it is at least the equivalent of making the husband of the adorable Emma, Mr. Nightly.

But M. Proust pointed out the queer

HIGH PLACES

fact that Stendhal, whenever he wishes to present to us the finest workings of his hero's consciousness, invariably takes him up into a high place, a lofty prison or a church tower. He lifts up Julien Sorel as well as Fabrice del Dongo. It is an odd effort of romantic symbolism. Probably it is as old as religion itself. The tower of Babel, the high places of Baal, the great towers of the Parsees, the Temptation in the Wilderness, perhaps even church spires themselves, all bear witness to the impulse to obtain release from earthly cares by climbing away from earth. The classical mind, which accommodates itself to the reality, either ignores or suppresses the impulse. With modern romanticism—it has been remarked many times before—the worship of mountains returned again to a world from which it had been banished for centuries.

Stendhal was a romantic, a peculiar one, but one of the greatest. And his romanticism shows itself perhaps most clearly in this impulse to put his heroes in high places. For the impulse seems to have been quite instinctive. His chosen natures had to be contemptuous of the practical world; therefore, quite literally, he made them look down upon it. Stendhal is an extreme case. But Balzac did much the same thing in that strange story *Seraphita*. When he was dealing, as he believed, with the highest mysteries of the human consciousness, he took Seraphitus-Seraphita into the Northern mountains. Quite recently Mr. D. H. Lawrence has obeyed the same instinct. In order that the final and mystical solution

HIGH PLACES

of their destinies may be accomplished, the two pairs of antagonistic lovers in *Women in Love* are wafted away from the English midlands to the snow-mountains of Switzerland.

But Stendhal's love of height—shall we call it altitudinarianism or hypsophily?—is the familiar romantic sentiment with a difference, just as he was a romantic with a difference. In him there is an element of precision in the vagueness, a touch of mathematical exactitude. In a general way it is this precision which gives him his extraordinary fascination. Could any one resist the charm of a man who wrote, and told us that he wrote, "Yesterday I was fifty," on the inside of his braces? Alas, it seems they can, although that act is deeply characteristic of Stendhal who carried the same spirit of naive exactness into all his books. He is perfectly precise about the height of Fabrice's tower. Three hundred and eighty steps led up to it. The church tower of the Abbé Blanès was "more than eighty feet high." What is more, it was an observatory, though the good abbé was more astrologer than astronomer.

Here Stendhal touches hands with Mr. Thomas Hardy. *Two on a Tower* plays also in a country observatory. It is a curious—yet curiously natural—method of eliminating the vagueness from a symbol of romantic sublimity. On the one hand height and the ineffable spaces of the universe, on the other the exactness of pure science. It gives a sense of security; the strength of romanticism is accepted,

HIGH PLACES

the weakness refused. Perhaps I am reading too much into a single clue, but it seems to me that this almost mathematical control of the delirium of height indicates a secret firmness in a writer's imaginative grasp. The vagueness of Seraphitus-Seraphita's mountains is a symptom of Balzac's surrender to Mesmer and Swedenborg; the Abbé Blanès's neat observatory corresponds to Stendhal's lucid mind. Comparing them, I feel justified in my private conviction that Stendhal was a better writer than his more famous contemporary. And when I think of *Two on a Tower,* immature though it is, my mind passes easily to the magnificent ending of *The Trumpet-Major,* when they look down from Portland Bill and gaze, not upon "illimitable leagues of sea," but upon Nelson's fleet sailing in certain order,

PENCILLINGS

ship by ship, to the glory of Trafalgar, and I know, as by a masonic sign, that we also have a writer who has imposed exactness upon the infinite.

DICKENS

I was struck by Mr. H. M. Tomlinson's remark, made in *The Times* a few days ago, that he was not surprised to find that a young writer and critic of his acquaintance thought that Dickens had gone the way of the wax-fruit. (Mr. Roger Fry, by the way, has told us that the wax-fruit are coming, have already come, back again.) I was surprised at Mr. Tomlinson's lack of surprise. My own impression is that in the last few years, let us say since 1914, there has been a marked revival of interest and admiration for Dickens among the younger generation. While Thackeray has been decidedly tarnished since he was put

PENCILLINGS

on the shelf, the splendour of Dickens, I fancy, now that he has been taken down again, shines as bright as ever.

I have a good memory for the evidences of a Dickens revival. I remember an intellectual dinner-party at which it was announced, without any manifest ill-effects upon the company, that the real test of literary taste was an admiration, not for Jane Austen (as some one had suggested), but for Dickens. And the reason given for making him the touchstone was that the lover of *Emma* might be an intellectual snob, while the lover of *David Copperfield* could not be. Then there was the letter of one who had been brought up in the strict Flaubert persuasion. He declared with the emphasis natural to a man who feels he has been deceived since childhood, that there was

DICKENS

more substance in Bella Wilfer alone than in all the created characters of the great Frenchman. He was extravagant, but I know what he meant.

Again, there is the striking fact that the finest essay on Dickens which has yet been written appeared only a few months ago in an organ of ultra-modern literature, the American *Dial*. Had it not been written by Mr. Santayana, it is possible it would not have squeezed its way through the narrow door. But there it undeniably was; and it was a masterpiece of profound and appreciative criticism. Those poor slaves of fashion who have hitherto had to read their Dickens in secret, if they read him at all, may now indulge themselves in the open. And for a final overwhelming proof, a proof by miracle, as it were, a proof of the *credo quia impossibile* kind, there is the acknowledgment by Mr. T. S. Eliot in the last number of *The Tyro* that Dickens is not altogether *vieux jeu*. "The critic," says Mr. Eliot, "is the person who has the power to discern what, in any work of literary art, takes its place, through its expression of the genius of its language, in European literature, and what is of purely local importance. (In the case of such a writer as Dickens, for example, the dissociation remains to be performed.)"

It is rather grim. Dickens is slipped into a parenthesis, squeezed between a pair of brackets as between a pair of forceps, tied down on the surgeon's table, and warned that a serious operation is necessary. But, at the cost of a certain expurgation his life can be saved. We need not despair

DICKENS

of him. We do not yet know, of course, how much will be cut away, or whether Dickens will be recognisable when he has been pruned into a European. We hope that Mr. Eliot means nothing worse than a careful excision of sentimentality. Even that pound of flesh might have to be taken, like Shylock's, from very near the heart. Still, there is hope. I seem to remember that Mr. Eliot made a much less hopeful diagnosis a year or two ago. Now that he has granted his provisional imprimatur, the most advanced young man may carry a copy of Pickwick in his pocket. If he is cross-questioned about the suspicious volume, he has only to reply that he is engaged in blue-pencilling the non-European parts.

Dickens is safe, so safe indeed that within the next twelve months he may become

PENCILLINGS

a snobism in his turn. The permissible portions may be printed in a limited edition with a cover design by ——, but that would be implied art criticism. Let us be content with the knowledge that the offence against art and intellect is no longer to know Dickens, but to be ignorant of him. I have read the signs with care, for the simple reason that, although I have floundered into most of the artistic snobisms of my time (and, I hope, floundered out again), I have never deserted Mr. Micawber. I may have been silent, but I have not deserted him. Not through any fundamental rectitude in my nature, but simply because of the accident that Pickwick was the first book I ever possessed. My copy began at page 19. I have never read those nineteen pages. They would not be real if I did. The

DICKENS

foundation of the Pickwick Club will always be a mystery to me.

Until the day when I read Mr. Gosse's *Father and Son,* I was persuaded that the behaviour Mr. Pickwick induced in me at the age of eight and nine was a clear proof of a peculiar madness. Even at that age I was half-ashamed of it. I used to begin to laugh before I had opened the book. (Perhaps that was as well, because the pages were so sticky that I should have lost precious time in opening them.) And I have never been able to read more than a few pages since then, because the helpless feeling of unquenchable Achæan laughter takes hold of me. I dare not let go my sanity; I am afraid of a second childhood. But Mr. Gosse reassured me, for he precisely described all my own

PENCILLINGS

alarming symptoms. "I felt myself to be in the company of a gentleman so extremely funny that I began to laugh before he began to speak; no sooner did he remark 'the sky was dark and gloomy, the air was damp and raw,' than I was in fits of hilarity. . . . Possibly," concluded Mr. Gosse, "I was the latest of the generation which accepted Mr. Pickwick with an unquestioning and hysterical abandonment." Some forty years later I was being plunged, at about the same age, into the same hysterical ecstasy. I cannot help believing that forty years hence it will happen again, and that the generations of childish Pickwick enthusiasts are perennial.

Afterwards come the phases of Dickens adulation. There is the year when Dora is woman, and the year when Squeers is

DICKENS

the devil incarnate; the year when Jonas Chuzzlewit makes our nights miserable, and Mrs. Gamp our days a delight; the year of confident maturity when we declare that *Our Mutual Friend* is Dickens's only work of art; the year after when we discover that even the death of Paul Dombey has an undiminished power to harrow our souls, though our teeth are set against its illicit compulsions; there is the year of Mrs. Jellyby, the year of Little Dorrit, the year of Sally Brass and the Marchioness. And then at last come the years when we give up the insoluble problem, when we are incapable of rejecting anything to which Dickens put his hand (unless it is *Hard Times*), when we simply know that we enter an amazing and extraordinary world, and that once we have abandoned ourselves to it

PENCILLINGS

the only wonder is that we could ever have been such fools as to remain deliberately outside, even for a single year.

Dickens is a baffling figure. There are moments when it seems that his chief purpose in writing was to put a spoke in the wheel of our literary æsthetics. We manage to include everybody but him; and we are inclined in our salad days to resent the existence of anybody who refuses to enter the scheme. That is why people tried to get rid of him by declaring that he was not an artist. It was an odd way of predicating non-existence. Now it is going out of fashion, I suppose because it did not have the desired effect of annihilating Dickens; and also perhaps because simple people asked why the books of a man who was not an artist should have this curious

DICKENS

trick of immortality. There was, alas, no answer. So we are beginning to discover that Dickens *was* an artist, but, of course, only in parts. When we have discovered which are the parts we shall breathe again.

THE GOLDEN PEN

Almost exactly a year ago the back cover of the *London Mercury* contained the advertisement of a publisher who quoted these words from a review. "To a knowledge of Russia probably unique, Mr. —— adds the advantage of writing with a pen that makes everything he says interesting." I will not give the name of the owner of the pen. So many people would write to him to borrow it, or at least to learn the name of the maker. I myself have refrained from pestering him, but I have been haunted by a vision of his pen ever since.

I have not got a pen of that kind. I was rather surprised to learn that Mr. —— had.

THE GOLDEN PEN

He must have acquired it recently; the last book of his that I read was not written with it. But I have often suspected that certain other writers had one, Mr. Bernard Shaw for instance, and Mr. Max Beerbohm and Miss Katherine Mansfield. And although I have never seen their pens, I have sometimes been tormented by a dream of one which would make not only my labours easy, but the results of them enchanting. The pen of my dream is a golden pen; it glides over a great sheet of white paper like crisp parchment; it is dipped into a crystal well of ink blacker than a raven's breast; and the lines it traces are as fine as those which Indian artists draw with an elephant's hair. And it seems to me that if all these things were mine, the thoughts of my brain would be as clean and fine and definite as

PENCILLINGS

they. An idea would rise before my mind like a bubble. I should only have to trace the outline. The bubble would break, the dust of its rainbow colouring would float down, settle on my ink before it was dry, and be imprisoned in it for ever.

That is extravagant; and yet is it so much more extravagant than some of the expedients actually devised by writers in the past to aid the mysterious process of expression? The quotation about the interesting pen sounds rather silly, but what could we have said if the publisher of the great Buffoon, as Mr. Shaw's childhood friend called him, had put in one of the advertisements for the *Histoire Naturelle*, "To a knowledge of nature probably unique, M. de Buffon adds the advantage of writing in a pair of cuffs which make

THE GOLDEN PEN

everything he says interesting"? If Buffon really found it impossible to work except in lace cuffs and a full-bottomed wig, the advertisement contains the simple truth. But of late there has been a tendency to throw suspicion on this account of the great naturalist's method. It has been said that the story was invented by a witty critic to describe the ornate majesty of Buffon's style. It may be so. But there is nothing in the least incredible in the story. It is indeed a very mild one compared with that extraordinary account of Schiller's habits which Goethe gave to Eckermann. Schiller happened to be out one day when Goethe came to see him. Goethe sat down at his friend's work-table. After a little while he felt faint, and noticed a curiously unpleasant smell, which he traced to a drawer of

Schiller's desk. He opened it, and was astonished to find that it was full of rotten apples. When he had recovered himself at the open window, Frau Schiller came in and explained that her husband insisted that his drawer should be kept full of rotten apples, "because the smell did Schiller good, and he could not live or work without it."

The medical expert might discover a difference in kind between Schiller's apples and Buffon's cuffs. He would probably say that Schiller's apples were like the opium of Coleridge and De Quincey, or the black coffee which Balzac so copiously drank, or the famous fumes which inspired the priestess of Delphi to prophesy from her tripod. But can any such line be really drawn between these aids to expression?

THE GOLDEN PEN

They are means used to produce a certain condition of quiescence in the physical being, to make the writer oblivious of the thousand physical sensations which distract his mind from the task of dragging the depths of unconscious memory. Narcotic drugs—and, I suppose, charitable wine must be included under that uncharitable name—are only a clearly marked species of a larger kind.

Consider the case of Dostoevsky. One of the few valuable pieces of information in his daughter's biography of him is that he could write only in absolutely clean clothes and linen. If there was a single spot or stain on his coat he was compelled to give up work until it had been removed. The presence of a stain affected him like a physical contamination. His mind was obsessed by it as by a direct physical sensation. I confess that this information concerning the painter of so many tremendous pictures of physical sordidness surprised me, just as I was surprised when I first saw a photograph of his incredibly neat study. It seemed more like the work-room of an ambassador than of the great novelist. My surprise was naive. I have since come to believe that it was precisely because physical degradation plays so great a part in the world of his literary creation that Dostoevsky had such an exaggerated nervous horror of it in reality. Dostoevsky was fighting with a devil. There was a hereditary taint in his family. It is this which accounts for the impressive reality of evil in his books, and for his fear of a single stain on his coat while writing them. Through a spot of

THE GOLDEN PEN

grease the devil might enter in. Clean linen was for him the whole armour of righteousness. When he put it on he was free.

That is a complicated case of psychology. Dostoevsky was a complicated man. There was much more behind his clean cuffs than Buffon's, though the motive for both was the same. They aimed at exorcising interruptions of the strange process of expression. Since the interruptions to which writers are peculiarly liable may differ widely, the means of defeating them may differ widely also. Most writers, no doubt, like quiet and isolation. But I know one—a writer with more than a streak of genius—who works most easily at the corner of a kitchen table while an animated conversation is going on over his head. The way his pen

PENCILLINGS

flew over the paper in the midst of this distracting babble used to amaze me. But that was simply because I myself would have been paralysed by his surroundings. One day I learned that his first lessons as a tiny schoolboy had been written on the kitchen table of a home where everything happened in the kitchen. So he had worked and read till he was twenty. The habit had become instinctive, until now the quiet which is the first condition of concentration to most of his tribe is to him a positive interruption. Just as the eye of imagination can glimpse the awful presence of a haunted family through Dostoevsky's agony at a stain, it can see through my friend's easy absorption at a kitchen table the whole history of a boyhood.

We seem to have wandered far from the

THE GOLDEN PEN

golden pen. But it is not so. The pen is but one among many of the conditions of literary expression, though it has been made the symbol of them all. The ideal pen is simply the pen which makes the actual operation of writing most unconscious. All that which helps to put the physical sensibility into abeyance is an aid to expression. I know a man who writes best at the top of a clean sheet of paper; when he gets lower down he begins to be distracted by what he has already written. To conquer this distraction requires an effort, and the effort is made at the cost of the proper effort of expression. I know another who is most at ease when writing on the backs of bills, newspaper margins, and the insides of envelopes. This was the man who replied to the demand of an agitated

PENCILLINGS

editor for a long overdue review that he had lost the book, but he enclosed another review in its place. The substitute review was written on the torn-out title page and end-papers of the book which was lost.

LITERATURE AND SCIENCE

A FRIEND of mine wrote to me the other day that "the sceptre has passed from literature to science." He is, of course, a man of science himself. And it seemed rather strange that he should use such a very literary phrase to express his triumph. It would have been more appropriate if he had sent me an equation. I should not have known what the equation meant. Perhaps that was the reason why he sent me a metaphor instead.

While I pondered his phrase it began to look to me like a barefaced contradiction in terms, and I wondered what kind of an equation would adequately express his satisfaction that literature had at last to play second fiddle to science. Even if an equation could be discovered with the proper nuance of "I told you so," what would be the pleasure for him if I did not appreciate it? No enemy is stronger than one who does not know he is beaten. And, to compare large things with small, would not the effect upon literature of the victory of science be precisely the same as the effect upon me of my defeat by an equation I could not understand? Literature may be shorn of its sceptre and its purple, but if there is no little boy to call out that the Emperor is naked, who will be the wiser? If nobody knows, who will care?

Nevertheless, since my friend is a brilliant man, I have done my utmost to extract a meaning from his phrase. I am sure that

LITERATURE AND SCIENCE

he means something more than to make my flesh creep. My flesh refuses to creep, but I want to know what he means. I suspect that his metaphor was badly chosen, and that he would have done better with two sceptres instead of one. Probably he meant that literature and science each had a sceptre, but the sceptre of science had of late become heavier and more imposing than the sceptre of literature. Literature now rules a little kingdom, while science rules a big one. But the kingdom of literature has certainly not been incorporated into the kingdom of science, nor is it likely to be. You might as well try to marry Boyle's Law to a bookcase.

But even if we take my friend to mean that science is now become a more important activity of the human mind than literature,

PENCILLINGS

is he saying more than that Boyle's Law is more valuable than a bookcase? And is not that a judgment without import, as the logicians say? Is he not like a man who insists on comparing the values of logarithms and love? And if we suppose he means only that at the present time abler minds are engaged in scientific discovery than in literary creation—a question exceedingly difficult to judge—the issue is not affected. Quite possibly our bridges are better built than our poems nowadays. As Socrates would have said, our bridges have more of the goodness of bridges than our poems have of the goodness of poems. But that does not mean that a bridge is more important than a poem, or a poem than a bridge.

   I suspect that what my friend has in his

LITERATURE AND SCIENCE

head is that the Einstein theory is a discovery of supreme philosophical importance; that for the first time the metaphysical doctrine of subjective idealism has been backed by a scientific proof; and that this will have a determining influence upon the future evolution of literature. The last of these propositions is the most doubtful. It is quite true that scientific theory does have an influence upon literary creation. But it has to be translated into emotional terms. In order to affect literature it has to affect our attitude to life. The theory of Natural Selection, emotionally interpreted as handing man over to the play of blind and uncontrollable forces, certainly gave a pessimistic tinge to the literature of the nineteenth century. The Copernican Revolution no doubt contributed to that emphatic isolation of the individual which is the beginning of modern romanticism. But we cannot say that the literature of the nineteenth century is either more or less important than Darwinism or the Copernican Revolution. There is no means of comparing them. What we can say is that the literature may wear better. When those two scientific theories have been exploded, as we are told they are being exploded now, the great books created by minds coloured by them will remain as fresh and valuable as ever.

For the truth of the matter surely is that there are very few emotional attitudes towards life which a man can truly and instinctively hold. He may believe life is painful and pitiful; he may believe it is glorious and splendid: he may confidently hope, he may continually despair, he may alternate between

LITERATURE AND SCIENCE

hope and despair. What his attitude will be is determined by many things: his heredity, his personal destiny, and to some degree by the scientific theories that obtain in his lifetime. A scientific theory which directly affects his hope of long life or immortality or better things to come, colours his mind and gives a twist to his sensibility. He becomes, if he is a writer, differently interested in life. In so far as either the Einstein theory or modern biology opens up new vistas of the significance or duration of human life, they will determine a change of tone in literature. Possibly the pessimism which still hangs about us like a cloud will be dissipated for a season. But it will return, simply because it is an eternal mode of the human spirit. And it may be dispelled without the cleansing

PENCILLINGS

wind of science, because optimism also is a natural mode of the human spirit.

Literature changes tone in obedience to these modes. But its substance is unchanged, for that is based on a delighted interest in human life and destinies. Science has no power over that interest, which is a gift of the gods like the genius of communicating it. When the man of science has power to determine or to change the structure of our minds, then literature may begin to fear him. By that time ordinary men will fear him also, and there will be a massacre of biologists. But till that day science can do no more to literature than to help to decide whether its vision of life shall be tinged with pity or happiness, resignation or confidence.

This may equally be decided by the

LITERATURE AND SCIENCE

indifference of the writer's mistress or his happiness in love. Science is only one of the things which colour the glass through which the writer looks at life; at present it can neither give nor take away the gift of seeing clearly through the glass; neither can it increase nor diminish the pleasure of those who take delight in what the writer can show them. The sceptre of science may be the more majestic. Beside its massy steel the rod of literature may appear slight and slender. We do not expect a magician's wand to look otherwise.

A NEW HUMANISM?

It may seem impertinent in me to reopen a subject which has already been discussed by abler pen than mine in this very place. But the subject and the occasion are important enough to justify every attempt to throw some light upon them. A message from Mr. Hardy to modern literature is nothing less than a Royal Command to examine our consciences. All other themes give way to this. Involuntarily I find myself turning over and over in my mind Mr. Hardy's verdict that in literature "we seem threatened by a new dark age."

The appearance is indubitable. We can imagine a stern observer saying, " The age

A NEW HUMANISM?

in literature, in art generally, is one of dissolution and disintegration. The creative forces which were on the verge of maturity before the war have been blighted by it; while those which emerged during the war are either listless or nihilistic or both. The war, like a knife, cut the thread of the English tradition. At the moment it seems impossible that it should be tied together again. There is no point of departure, no solid rock of social or religious security on which the present generation can begin to build. From the highest ability to the lowest it is infected by a desire for crude or refined sensationalism. This is the age, in literature, of scraps without coherence, of boredom which can be relieved only by the braying of a jazz-band, of a frenzied eagerness to uncover our father's nakedness and our own."

All this, from one point of view, is true. It is also more true of other countries than our own. Russia has been in the same condition now for nearly twenty years. France is much more deeply bitten by Dadaism than England has been by its equivalent or imitation. Germany is more seriously affected still. Even in America it seems to have a deeper hold than it has among us. Still, we must admit that a great part of the youth of the world is given over to an exasperated cynicism. Its audience is not large. The audience for youth never is. The fact that its productions seldom reach beyond a small circle cannot be invoked to prove that the condition is not real and serious.

A NEW HUMANISM?

Real and serious it may be; yet perhaps not so desperate as it must inevitably appear to Mr. Hardy. Mr. Hardy cannot know how hopeful is the reverence felt towards himself by the generation which seems hopeless to him. And even if this modern reverence for Mr. Hardy is still accompanied by an unadvised neglect of other great figures of the Victorian era, the reverence is the thing that matters. Amid the pathetic extravagances of genius or talent, or the flippant emptiness which apes them, a younger observer may discover in this respect for Mr. Hardy signs of a hunger, if not for religion, for the peace of an attitude of mind which might with some truth be called religious.

For a crucial example of this reverential tinge of the modern conciousness, take the work of Mr. Lytton Strachey. I remember how those who had appreciated only the wittily destructive portions of *Eminent Victorians* rubbed their hands in delighted anticipation of *Queen Victoria*. Now, the cynical Mr. Strachey would fairly let himself go, with the real Aunt Sally for his target. Mr. Strachey did nothing of the kind. If ever a great character was handled tenderly, with an insight tempered by affection, it was the Queen Victoria of his biography. And it is surely not too much to say that he changed the mind not only of his contemporaries, but of his seniors about the central figure of a great era.

Not that we pay Mr. Strachey's generation the compliment of regarding him as typical of it; but the evident movement of his mind from a more or less destructive cynicism

A NEW HUMANISM?

towards a positive and valuable humanism is characteristic. I would—if the apology were not to some extent *pro domo meâ*—point out the change in temper which distinguishes Miss Katherine Mansfield's *Garden Party* from her *Bliss*. And above all I would emphasise the significance of the homage paid to Tchehov as an artist and a man, and of the intimate appeal made to the modern mind by his combination of æsthetic and morality. It is possible to be cheated by one's eagerness to catch a certain tone; but to me the signs, though small, are manifold of a movement towards what can only be described as a new humanism.

These signs will not be visible to those who look for a definite religious revival. The sequence of catastrophes which has driven so many Russian authors and men of science into mystical religion has no parallel in our own discomfitures; neither has the English mind that underlying tendency towards mystic self-abnegation which is permanent in the Russian. If, as we are sometimes assured there is, a religious revival in modern England, it does not seem to touch modern literature, save in the persons who were more or less completely formed before the war. What we have instead is an instinctive attempt to overcome that divorce between complete rationality and the religious sense which Mr. Hardy so clearly discerns and so justly deplores.

To some the Einstein theory may show the way of reconciliation. To others—and I fancy modern writers will be found among these—it may come more simply

A NEW HUMANISM?

in a new recognition of the order of human values and a loyalty to the highest. As the most famous of modern French poets, M. Paul Valéry, said the other day, there is still room for a mysticism of life itself. To prevent the stunting of wisdom by the growth of knowledge, to know where disintegration should end and positivism begin, to feel what is moribund in our tradition and what is permanently vital, to avoid the condition eloquently described by Lucretius as *"propter vitam vivendi perdere causas,"* and wittily by the German professor as " Emptying the baby with the bath "—knowledge of this kind is mystical in the sense that no ratiocination can supply it. But it is rational also because the reason admits its own incompetence. Complete rationality will always open a door on to the wisdom which

PENCILLINGS

is beyond knowledge. But when the struggles of a generation towards complete rationality are precipitated by the agony of a world, they are so violent that they seem like death-pangs to the detached onlooker. Nevertheless, we believe they are growing pains.

THE CURÉ OF WANGS

I HAVE made a literary discovery. That will suggest at the very least a first edition of Keats for sixpence, or an unknown letter by Dr. Johnson tucked away in a folio history. To some it may appear positively misleading. But they are those to whom "a literary discovery" must necessarily mean an event in bibliophily. I have no grudge against the bibliophiles. I pretend to despise their curiosity and keenness, but at heart I envy them their knowledge. Still more I envy them the uncanny instinct which enables them to pull out of the three-penny box under my very eyes the book which may possibly be a rarity. The

PENCILLINGS

chances are a hundred to one that it is not; the chances are also a hundred to one that if it is the bibliophile will get it. There is a swiftness and economy in his behaviour which I admire.

But it is an admiration which has nothing to do with literature. Books are merely the *corpus vile* upon which this instinctive and scientific precision is exercised. Literary discovery is altogether different. Probably no one has ever been a penny the richer for making one; and very often, if the discovery is one of the first importance, his anxiety to share it with the world will be the cause of much vexation of spirit to himself. During his efforts to convert the indifferent, he will be frowned on as a crank; and when the indifferent are converted, his discovery will be reckoned as

THE CURÉ OF WANGS

a commonplace and rewarded with ingratitude.

Luckily, my discovery is not of the epoch-making kind. I shall not even have the satisfaction of helping an unknown author to fame. Already in 1914 the sales of the book I have found were comparable with the sales of *If Winter Comes.* 220,000 copies of *Bonnes et Mauvaises Herbes,* by Jean Künzle, curé of Wangs, near Sargans, in Switzerland, had been printed ten years ago. It is a little book of eighty pages, and is apparently the only reading of the landlady of the remote Swiss inn where I am staying. When one's books are limited to a score of old familiar faces, one is grateful for anything in print; and much more than grateful for a Herbal written by a man of character and charm.

PENCILLINGS

My eye was caught first by his description of the nettle. " The nettle is like a rather rough man, who nevertheless has a heart and is ready in case of need to sacrifice his life to save his neighbour's." That was enough. It reminded me of St. François de Sales, who was indeed almost a countryman of the curé's, and I sat down to read the book through. It is in the most fragrant sense of the word a simple book, fortified by a strange and rare combination of Christian charity and wit. Indeed, the curé's attitude towards " the bad herbs " sometimes recalls a St. Francis who was even greater than he of Sales, for he finds a peculiar satisfaction in rescuing weeds from obloquy and contempt. " The Equisetum," he says, " is detested by those who have to pull it up. They consign it to

THE CURÉ OF WANGS

all the devils. But many of its detractors have for years been resting in peace round the church. If they had gathered it in due season and made use of it, they would still be among the living, and perhaps would have reached the age of crows, who never make their wills before they have seen ninety summers and as many winters."

That is surely a charming piece of writing; and the charm endures when the curé appears as the critic of modern civilisation. He cannot abide neurasthenia. "Every one with a certain amount of culture," he says, "thinks it fashionable to be a little neurasthenic. If the doctor wants to gain the confidence of a lady of high rank, he has only to tell her that she is neurasthenic. Then she finds his bitterest pills delicious; she tightens her corset a little more, and stays up an hour longer reading novels; she drinks her black coffee a little stronger and subscribes to some more fashion papers. These people are as proud of their neurasthenia as the cows and goats are of their bells." And listen to this description of the spoiled Swiss peasant who returns from seeking his fortune abroad. "There are people who used to tie up parcels or wash bottles abroad. Now they refuse to carry anything heavier than their umbrella, which must not weigh more than a pound. And as often as not they forget that."

The curé cannot stomach modern poetry any better than modern civilisation. In a paragraph on the virtues of porridge he quotes Hebel, the working-man poet of Basle, who wrote over a hundred years ago:

THE CURÉ OF WANGS

"Children, come and eat your porridge. Let yourselves grow big and strong."

And the curé continues, in a burst of confession, "I cannot endure modern poets, or pianos, or the educational laws—these evidences of an over-excited civilisation; but I allow myself to quote Hebel because he cannot be included among these cloudy poets who sing only of decayed trees and light-living ladies."

Return to Nature and God's remedies, says the curé, who belongs to the race of Rousseau's Savoyard Vicar. Don't coddle your children. The barefoot child is twice as strong as the one who "even in midsummer wears shoes and stockings as a sign of nobility." Then he gives a picture of the after-life of the stockinged Fauntleroys. "They are always white as a flour-sack,

PENCILLINGS

light as a feather, and brittle as porcelain. No sooner are they out of school in winter than they have to be taking medicine, and be swaddled in bands and coverings like poachers. They are racked with anæmia, headaches and toothaches eternal. If these dolls enter into marriage, their husbands will have music to last them their lives, for they will have in their houses organs which play plaintive tunes and have an octave added with the birth of every child." That is the authentic note of Burton's *Anatomy*. And one can find Burton's quaint vigour of speech in the chapter on the virtues of absinthe—the plant, not the liqueur—" If any one is as green as a frog, thin as a poplar, and cannot see his own shadow; if his weight and good humour dwindle every day, he can try to take a spoonful of absinthe tea

THE CURÉ OF WANGS

every two hours." "He can *try*" is a masterstroke.

The curé is not unfriendly to the doctor; but he is the declared enemy of "the false science of the eighteenth (not the nineteenth) century, which rejected all that it did not understand." Chief among these things were the beneficent properties of plants. The Encyclopædists did not know, as the curé does, that every bad herb is good for something. He does not pretend to understand how they work their effects, which he is ready to ascribe to "radioactivity or some other power that God has given them." But he is certain that they were set in the world by God for the use of his children. Most of his human children have forgotten how to use them; but the animals remember. The truth is with the animals and the men of old. "The false savants can go home to Babylon."

The curé is gentle in his triumph, he does not exult over his enemies; but he cannot refrain from breaking every now and then into praise of the merciful works of God. And perhaps most characteristic of all is the little paragraph with which he ends his chapter on "Pains of the Heart." After giving the healing herbs, he says, "If it is great trouble, care, or anxiety which causes your pain at heart, go and find the priest of your parish, who has ready for you a marvellous plant, 'the wheat of the elect.' That will do you good." I am no lover of sermons; but I would go a long way—even to Wangs near Sargans—to hear my curé preach.

THE PROBLEM OF SIZE

THE other day I listened to a famous French poet lecturing on the ideas of Edgar Allan Poe. Unfortunately, the thread of his discourse rapidly disappeared into the metaphysical mazes of *Eureka,* and only the most casual loop was thrown about that one of Poe's ideas which has had a very remarkable influence upon the development of modern French poetry. I mean his theory that the unit of poetry must be fixed by the reader's capacity of attention, and that the limits of a poem must accord with the limits of a single movement of intellectual apprehension and emotional exaltation. A long poem, said Poe, was really only a sequence of short ones; and it would be a good thing (he thought) if it did not pretend to be anything else.

The theory—though it is more pretentious or more " philosophical "—reminds one of Mr. H. G. Well's definition of the short story as a fiction that can be read in a quarter of an hour. Poe's " poem " is likewise a set of verses that can be compassed by a single movement of the mind. The effect of the beginning is not lost before you reach the end. You hold it, as it were, completely in your hand; the mind's eye can embrace it in a single glance. There is nothing very original in the principle, which determined the most famous of all European poetical forms—the sonnet, and has apparently always dominated the poetry of China and Japan. But Poe was the first to formulate

THE PROBLEM OF SIZE

it as an absolute law, and Baudelaire followed him.

There is room here for some work by the experimental psychologists. We invite them to determine the ideal length of a poem. Does it lie somewhere in the large space between the seventeen syllables of a *hokku* and the hundred and forty of a sonnet, or is the ordinary attention capable of a yet longer flight before coming to earth? These are questions not unworthy of scientific solution. But there is perhaps a more immediate interest in the general principle which Poe applied, namely that the size of a work of literature should be determined by the capacity of the audience. Aristotle had no doubt about it. The play or the picture must not be too big to be grasped as a whole at a first hearing or seeing.

PENCILLINGS

From that comfortable and human point of view we have travelled far. *The Ring and the Book* and *The Dynasts, War and Peace* and the *Forsyte Saga,* make the Aristotelian ideal look small indeed.

Still, we may fairly say (if we believe there is something in Poe's contention) that just as a long poem is a sequence of short poems, a big story is a number of little ones. There is a constant ebb and flow of interest, a continual heightening and flagging of attention. And if we admit this as a psychological fact, we may begin to wonder whether that technical movement in English fiction which was inspired by Flaubert and culminated in Henry James was altogether well-advised. These exponents of the art of fiction imagined themselves confronted by an audience of

THE PROBLEM OF SIZE

intellectual heroes, whose attentions never flagged and whose memories never failed. This "hypothetical intelligent man" was acutely sensitive to any shifting of the angle of presentation; he became restive if he once suspected that all the events recorded in a novel could not have been present to the same consciousness. He was the devil of a fellow.

The only thing against him is that he does not exist. And that omission of his more than anything else will save us from fiction that demands as much concentration as a three volume treatise on Neo-Hegelian metaphysics. No one really pays much attention now to the subtle problems which tormented Henry James, simply because no one would earn any gratitude by solving them. Even the attempt to solve them calls for a private income. But the fact of the matter is that even the most intelligent reader of a long novel is grateful for a pause, a respite, a breathing-place. The episodic novel provides them naturally. We can get through *Tom Jones* or *The Pickwick Papers* with plenty of wind to spare. Nor do we harbour any grudge against a writer who interrupts a novel that is not episodic with digressions and asides.

Indeed, I am not at all sure that those novelists who were not afraid of saying " dear reader " every now and then, or of giving their personal views of a chance topic, or even of their own created characters, had not a better instinct for the conditions of their craft than the purist who banished them from the republic of art. A novel should give us the illusion of life, it is true.

THE PROBLEM OF SIZE

But we do not greatly mind if the illusion is broken now and then. When Anthony Trollope pops up and says, " Don't worry. Eleanor Bold won't marry either Mr. Slope or Bertie Stanhope," our head may be contemptuous but our heart puts up with it perfectly well. And when at the end of *Barchester Towers* the genial sinner flings all his cards on the table and asks, " Do I not myself know that I am at this moment in want of a dozen pages, and that I am sick with cudgelling my brain to find them?" we lift an eyebrow perhaps, but we read placidly on.

That, we are told, is not art. Neither, then, is *Tristram Shandy* art, nor *Jacques le Fataliste,* where Diderot is for ever asking you and me what he shall do with Jacques next. But art is a very fluid conception which takes a new shape every ten years or so. It is safer to replace the abstract notion by the reality of books which we know have lasted because we still enjoy them. And if we look a little closely into the reality we shall discover that in their go-as-you-please fashion these novelists were instinctively obeying the law formulated by Poe, and we reach the not unamusing paradox that Poe's law applied to poetry has become the gospel of the straiter sect of literary artists; applied to prose fiction it has become their anathema.

For the essence of Poe's law is not that poems should be short, but that the reader's capacity of attention should be treated as an essential factor in determining a literary form. And that is precisely what the Victorian novelist instinctively did. He

THE PROBLEM OF SIZE

felt that the reader would find it a relief if his attention was occasionally diverted. It would not do any harm if he had been successful in endowing his characters with a life of their own; they would continue to exist in spite of the interruption, as a play exists in spite of an interval. If they were lifeless, nothing could save them, not even the quintessence of art. And perhaps the Victorian novelist did well in building upon an actual instead of a hypothetical audience. He allowed for his reader; and in consequence he is read.

ON DEPENDABLE WRITERS

IN a recent volume of essays Mr. Hewlett complained that he was never allowed to change his rôle. He had begun by swashing the buckle in fiction, and the public took it hardly if he tried to do anything else. From the writer's personal point of view the public is, like the law to Mr. Bumble, an ass; but socially, in trying to confine the writer to a single genre it acts wisely. Feeling that the literary artist is too volatile a person altogether, it seeks to pin him down, to make him *be* something as definite as a maker of buttons or gramophones. Once he is fairly identified, his name and address noted, and the quality of his goods

ON DEPENDABLE WRITERS

remarked and approved, it expects him to supply a dependable article "as last time" and not to go gallivanting off into sidelines which it is accustomed to buy from a different establishment.

In trying to squeeze the Protean soul of the writer into a single mould, the public is blindly seeking to impart to him its instinctive and ancestral wisdom that man as a rule does best by squarely facing limitations until they become second nature to him. Just as blindly it overlooks the fact that quite often the writer is much less interested in doing something supremely well than in satisfying the demands of his own capricious nature. That, it feels, is very bad for him, and it shows what it thinks of his escapades by blandly ignoring them. At last, like Lesbia's sparrow, after hopping about hither and thither, the writer becomes aware of the growing vacancy, and *ad solam dominam usque pipilabit.*

The public, in this rôle of instinctive mentor, embodies a vital principle that is in each one of us. We like to know where we are, and that depends upon our knowing where everybody else is. Mugwumps, sceptics, people who see both sides of a question, men without prejudices, make us uneasy. They are incalculable and lacking in ballast. A prejudice that we can allow for is much more dependable than a suspension of judgment that we can't. So we turn a blind eye to the signals which a writer hoists against our expectation and sail on to meet him at the accustomed rendezvous. If he is not there, so much the worse for him.

ON DEPENDABLE WRITERS

The writer who wants to be versatile had better begin early. Then by the time he is gray-haired and rather anxious to slip into a comfortable groove, he may have the reputation of turning up anywhere. Then he can be as serious and steady as he likes; his regularity will only be one more of his delightful whimsies. But the penalty attached to this freedom is heavy; he must have been ignored during most of his lifetime. If he wants to be observed and charted, he must stand in the same place; or, if he refuses to stand in the same place and yet insists upon being observed he must face the necessity of leaving a dummy in the bed while he slips out into the street to note the qualities of people. If he does not provide the dummy himself, the public will.

PENCILLINGS

Contrast the destinies of those two related spirits, Samuel Butler and Bernard Shaw. Butler's fame has been almost wholly posthumous, and we attend to him (now that we have begun to attend to him) in all his capacities. He never had a rôle to fill, or rather he disappointed expectation at the first time of asking, and so he was never labelled. Bernard Shaw, on the other hand, has taken good care that he should be attended to since birth, and he has paid for the attention. He is the paradoxical playwright or he is nothing. The rest is the froth we blow off the tankard before taking a pull. Yet in this froth are contained two personalities at least which would in isolation have made the fortune of another man. There is the best living writer of plain English prose, and the most original and

ON DEPENDABLE WRITERS

profound of modern literary critics. But there is no room for them on the label, and away, like the froth, they go.

Perhaps some one will take in hand the task of compiling a book of Bernard Shaw's literary criticism, giving half of it to his statements of general principles, and the other half to his criticism of Shakespeare. It might help to clear the heads of those many people who still imagine that since Matthew Arnold died there has been no criticism in England. Into the first half he shall put this: "A true original style is never achieved for its own sake.... Effectiveness of assertion is the Alpha and Omega of style. He who has nothing to assert has no style and can have none: he who has something to assert will go as far in power of style as its momentousness and his

PENCILLINGS

conviction will carry him. Disprove his assertion after it is made, yet its style remains." That takes its place naturally among the dozen or so statements made about style which quiver in the gold.

The story of Shaw and Shakespeare is almost fantastic. Shaw is the finest critic of Shakespeare we have had since ———. The finest critic of Shakespeare, as you have noticed, has always to be the finest critic of Shakespeare since some one or other. In order not to offend against the tradition, I leave the blank to be filled *ad lib.*, with the warning that Shaw is a better critic of Shakespeare than either Goethe or Coleridge, because he is not hypnotised. But there is no room for this on the label. All that it will hold is "Better than Shakespeare?" And so Bernard Shaw remains

ON DEPENDABLE WRITERS

the man who is irreverent to Shakespeare, whereas he should be the man who stands up to Shakespeare.

Listen to his irreverence. "This is what is the matter with Hamlet all through: he has no will except in his bursts of temper. Foolish Bardolaters make a virtue of this after their fashion; they declare that the play is the tragedy of irresolution; but all Shakespeare's projections of the deepest humanity he knew have the same defect. Their character and manners are life-like; but their actions are forced on them from without, and the external force is grotesquely inappropriate except where it is quite conventional, as in the case of Henry V." That is criticism worth having, sentences you carry about for days in your head, hammering and trying them, testing

PENCILLINGS

them by your own experience. And yet the other day Mr. Ezra Pound, apparently annoyed because Bernard Shaw had not bowed the knee to *Ulysses*—there is, by the way, some really imaginative Shakespeare criticism in that book—declared that he was "ninth-rate." A ninth-rate playwright? A ninth-rate prose writer? A ninth-rate critic? Then, oh, to be a tenth-rater in any of these things!

WHAT IS STYLE?

THE distinguished critic who writes in the pages of *The New Statesman* over the name of Affable Hawk has pounced upon me, affably enough, but nevertheless pounced upon me for holding up to admiration Bernard Shaw's dictum that the Alpha and Omega of style is effectiveness of assertion. It is (he says) but a half-truth, and what is worse, it is the half of the truth which had best be left in darkness at the present juncture. He thinks that we have more than enough writers nowadays who have, or think they have, something to say, and trust to its momentum to carry them along, with consequences that are often disastrous.

PENCILLINGS

What we need, he concludes, is the craftsman of words, the master of technique.

My impression is that the Hawk has swooped at a shadow. Bernard Shaw's dictum, though I find it admirable, is not my own. To square with my own convictions it needs to be expanded or at least interpreted. But even without expansion or interpretation, it has the virtue common to all Mr. Shaw's literary criticisms: it is provocative of thought, and therefore admirable. Any one who wants to discover what he means by style could hardly do better than begin with Mr. Shaw's sentence. When he has made trial of the definition by many passages in which he instinctively recognises the quality of style, he will find out what adjustments are necessary to fit it to his own experience.

WHAT IS STYLE?

Probably not many. He may find difficulty in the word "assertion." What, he might ask, was Milton asserting when he wrote "Sabrina fair"? And at first there seems to be no answer. But afterwards he will consider that if what Milton was asserting in that magical poem could be communicated in words other than those of the poem itself, the poem would be a failure. For the poem is our datum. It is precisely because we feel that there is in its language a manifest inevitability, because we are instinctively aware that not a word can be changed without injury, that we have originally ascribed to it the quality of style. If we could say that it was an assertion of this or that definite proposition, its inevitability would immediately be destroyed. For it is an axiom in literature that there cannot be two effective assertions of the same thing. There can be only one. That is the true meaning of the doctrine of *le mot juste*.

It may be urged that if "assertion" is to be interpreted in this large sense, the word becomes a shadow. But why? "Assertion" is a better, a more effective word, for the creative process in literature than "statement," because it suggests the driving force behind a true style. Something is imposed upon the reader; he is not permitted to escape the experience the writer intends for him. The phrase, "effective assertion," suggests this element of compulsion, of foreordained reaction.

It may also be objected that Mr. Shaw did not intend his phrase precisely in this sense, and that he meant by "assertion"

WHAT IS STYLE?

something nearer to what we ordinarily understand by the word. I do not doubt it. Has not Mr. Shaw himself plainly told us that he is more sympathetic to the writer of conviction than the writer of apprehension, to a Bunyan than to a Shakespeare? But that does not in the least prevent his phrase from bearing a wider meaning. It is a good phrase, forged by a writer who knows his business and has thought about it. Like a good bridge, it will carry twice the weight it was designed to bear.

Still, if we say the assertion of " Sabrina fair " is the poem itself, are we not emptying the phrase of meaning? Not really. The poem, having style, is an effective assertion of something, and though it is impossible for us to describe the thing asserted apart from the terms of the assertion, we are, nevertheless, conscious of it. We are aware of the perceptions which impelled Milton to write and determined his poem. The sheer, crystalline quality—" the glassy, cool, translucent wave "—corresponds to a vision of a kind we know. In fact, we do recognise in the assertion a something asserted; the assertion gives form and shape to dimmer perceptions of our own. But it can only do that because it is an effective assertion. It has the power to awaken a single complex of emotions within us. We have had emotions like them before, but never so powerfully, never with such a sense of their unity: before, they were dishevelled, now they are coherent; before, they were vague, now they are clear. But by the dulled memories of our own

WHAT IS STYLE?

perceptions we can distinguish the bright ones from which Milton began.

The process of making an assertion effective is the process of style. Mr. Shaw's dictum is an unconscious condensation of Stendhal's definition of style, which seems to me the most pregnant of all. " Le style est ceci: ajouter à une pensée donnée toutes les circonstances propres à produire tout l'effet que doit produire cette pensée." And I cannot for the life of me see that this is merely a half-truth, much less that it is the half of the truth of which we stand in no present need. We are always in need of it, and we never need anything else. It is not the assertion that makes the style, but the effectiveness of it. But on the one hand you cannot make an effective assertion effective without technique. To the writer of genius, no doubt, technique comes chiefly by instinct; but even when the genius is greatest I believe there is an immense amount of half-conscious experimentation. What I do not believe is that any considerable writer ever learned much of his technique from other writers without becoming perceptibly hidebound.

At this point inevitably some one will face me with Stevenson's phrase about "the sedulous ape." If Stevenson really played "the sedulous ape," he suffered for it. No man's habit of thought or vision (if he is to be an original writer) is sufficiently like another's for him to imitate his technique except at his own peril. In a real sense, of course, the writers who have gone before him are part of his inheritance; their coinages are part of his common currency,

WHAT IS STYLE?

their discoveries his tradition. He has more colours on his palette than Chaucer, but the only way he can ever learn how to use them is by having something urgent to say, something that must be said effectively or not at all. Then, under pressure of necessity, he evolves a technique that is as much his own as his vision. The more securely he possesses his content, the more securely he possesses his technique.

I do not think, therefore, that because I believe effectiveness of assertion to be the Alpha and the Omega of style, I can fairly be accused of advocating hot-gospelling or holy-roaring as the short road to good writing. Assertions are not effective because they are loud. Neither will apprehensions or convictions by themselves make a man a writer; but no man can become a writer without them. And it seems to be true that if they are strong and individual enough in a man, he will find the way to utter them effectively, whereas no amount of sedulous apery or word-mosaic will make a writer of the dilettante bellelettrist. As Mr. Shaw has said, " A true, original style is never achieved for its own sake." Style is a means to an end, and only when its end is achieved can we perceive its beauty: indeed, its beauty is only the name we give to our recognition that its end has been achieved.

MANNERS AND MORALITY

THE other day a youthful critic gave it as his opinion that Mr. Galsworthy had failed in *The Forsyte Saga* because he is a propagandist, and he added that "no great novelist has ever been that." It was rash of him to put his head into chancery, and no doubt he has been properly pummeled for it by now. Anyhow, I am not going to do it. Indeed, I should have forgotten all about him if I had not read on the same day in Mr. Edward Garnett's *Friday Nights,* that exhilarating record of the unselfish enthusiasms of a great literary pioneer, that a work of literature was ruined by the presence of a moral intention in the writer's mind.

The statement is odd in itself, and doubly odd on Mr. Garnett's lips, for if ever there was a literary critic who was inspired by an intense moral passion for fine literature it is he. Moreover, any one who reads his book (and they should be legion) will discover that the flame of moral passion glows at the heart of literature as Mr. Garnett conceives it. The great writer and the good are alike animated by a devouring appetite for truth; if they are not, they are neither great nor good. If the desire to discern and to communicate the truth about life —a vague phrase that we all understand— be not a moral intention, I do not know what a moral intention is. This loyalty to an ideal of spiritual honesty is the power

MANNERS AND MORALITY

which compels the true writer to make the sacrifice he is continually making; it is the fire which refines the gold of his thoughts and perceptions from the dross, and redeems them from decay.

As I began to wonder why writers and critics at the present day are so afraid of this word moral, I remembered a sentence in Coleridge's *Table Talk* which has always seemed to supply a golden thread to guide us through this labyrinth of confusion about morality in literature. Coleridge was speaking of Rabelais, and he said: "The morality of his work is of the most refined and exalted kind; as for the manners, to be sure, I cannot say much." There the vital distinction is made plain; that is why Rabelais endures for ever, while a contemporary sculdudderist like Beroaldus de

PENCILLINGS

Verville is forgotten. We can translate, or expand, Coleridge's sentence thus. The essential morality of Rabelais's attitude to life is of the highest; the habits and behaviour of the characters through whom he expresses this attitude are socially dubious. And we may add that so far as we can see they had to be socially dubious, for we can discover no other way of expressing precisely what Rabelais had to express.

People are always confusing, and it is a tribute to the creative power of the writer that they do confuse, the morality of the behaviour of the writer's characters with the morality of his work. They are, of course, totally different things. Falstaff is a non-moral character, but he is a moral creation. Every character that we feel to be typical, to be in his individual existence

MANNERS AND MORALITY

symbolic of one of the great forces which we vaguely discern at work in human life, is a moral creation, and the work of every writer who can create such a character has morality. Dickens is moral, not because he drowned Steerforth, but because he created Micawber. And if it be urged that a doctrine of this kind is a licence to a writer to outrage the social morality of his age, the reply is that the age can look after itself. The morality of a given society is not the morality of the writer of genius; he would simply not be a writer of genius if it were. But if he is a writer of common sense as well—and the finest genius is well-seasoned with common sense—he will recognise that he has to take account of the morality of his time. He will see that it is an instrument of good, though perhaps a clumsy one; and he will certainly know that it is better to have a book published than suppressed, to be out of prison than in it.

Great writers come to terms with their age; that is, they express their morality in manners that are tolerable to their contemporaries. Sometimes the problem is easy, sometimes hard; but they solve it. Dostoevsky had to sacrifice an important chapter of *The Possessed* to the censor in Russia, where the moral censorship was always trivial, on moral grounds. He made no fuss about it, and we might have forgotten about it had not the Bolshevists lately unearthed it from the archives. The difficulties caused by the moral enthusiasm of the official and unofficial censors of literature are by no means so great a trial to the writer

MANNERS AND MORALITY

as they are often represented to be. Still, no one would deny that they are troublesome and unfairly hampering, or that they generally involve the writer whose morality is impassioned, while the writer whose morality is as sordid as his manners almost always manages to escape.

One of the best ways of minimising this injury to literature would be to revive this lost distinction between morality and manners. It would also make it easier to hit hard and promptly those writers who take advantage of the fact that the manners of a book are no indication of its morality, to present us in the name of "art" with the morality of the brothel disguised as the manners of "the aristocracy." There is simply no way of saying these things with half the pungency and directness that the clear distinction between these two words allows. A writer once told me, when I was beginning to earn my living with a fountain pen, that the quickest way to success was to write a novel for the special purpose of having it "banned by the libraries." He seems to have been right; for he certainly has gained a great deal of money by his method. I have often since regretted that I had not then the distinction between morality and manners at my finger-ends. It would have enabled me to reply to him in a way which would have satisfied me, though it might not have affected him.

We are much at the mercy of words; they govern our thoughts more often than they obey them. The Victorian age, which passed its discreet sponge over the distinction

MANNERS AND MORALITY

between manners and morality, made a confusion where there was a clearness. So it happened that writers became shy of the word morality, and highly moral people began to shiver at the suggestion of a moral intention. The word had been so often used against a piece of honest literature that they had become afraid of it. It is time that writers took it into their own hands and made a weapon against their enemies and the traitors within their camp. They would be all the better for the exercise; and they would discover clearly what at present they feel only vaguely, that a work of literature, if it is to last, must have morality, simply because morality means significance, the power to engage the highest attention of man with feelings and thoughts derived from the faithful contemplation of human life. To avoid morality is not to be bold, or advanced, or artistic; it is simply, in the long run, to be uninteresting.

MORALITY AGAIN

I HAVE been taken, both publicly and privately, to task for saying that morality is essential to literature. The public dissentients prophesy, with an impressive foreknowledge, that I am heading, unconsciously, perhaps, but certainly, straight to the damnation of the doctrine that the writer must take care to be good and let who will be clever; the private suggest that there may be a confusion in my thought. Examine your assumptions, they say to me, and hint that I may find things I do not care to look upon. Even the kindest of my critics is distressed by my use of the word morality; it seems to him that it is almost a treachery to the ideal of literature. The gate is being opened to those enemies who insist that a book must have a "message," or that it must be "happy," or that its characters must not offend against the rules of society. "We *must*," says my friend—and there is a note of agony in his voice—"we *must* find another word."

Well, perhaps we must. For tactical reasons only. Perhaps it is impossible in this age of the dominion of the phrase, when words seem to exert powers which do not belong to them, to trust that people will hold asunder the morality which is necessary to enduring literature, and the morality which is, at least in part, the product of social convention. Obviously if the belief that morality is necessary to literature can be interpreted as the first

MORALITY AGAIN

symptom of the doctrine that goodness is everything and cleverness nothing, it is dangerous to use the word too often. It is, as they say, asking for trouble. The pity is that confusion should be inevitable where it seems unnecessary.

Moreover, it is disheartening to find that work once done, and well done, should have continually to be done over again. For all this discussion is by no means new; and perhaps the oddest thing is that the author to whom most of the recent generation of believers in Art for Art's sake regarded as their master and prophet, was perfectly clear on the subject. Walter Pater's critical work seems to have been forgotten; he has become a classic and suffered the fate of a classic, which is, to remain unread, or, if read, to be read with reverentially misted eyes. Otherwise it is hard to see why we should be perpetually threatened with the false dilemma: art, on the one hand, morality on the other; choose which you like, but both you cannot have. For ever we are being taken back to the elements. Apparently there is a kind of nostalgia which prevents us from taking advantage of what has been done before us. I sat for many years at the feet of a mathematical master who, whenever I forgot (as I invariably did forget) the elementary propositions of geometry of conic sections, used to give out a kind of despairing roar: " Two Peter, two, twenty-two! " The constant return of the old childish dilemma seems to call for the same reply.

For Pater distinguished clearly in literature between what he called qualities of

MORALITY AGAIN

mind and qualities of soul. The qualities of mind are, in the largest sense, qualities of technique. They find expression in formal beauty, in coherent structure, in economy of language; they are the sign of the constructive intelligence without which a complete and perfect expression of the writer's apprehension of life is impossible. Qualities of soul, on the other hand, are qualities of the apprehension itself, rendering it sympathetic to some, alien to others. They are the cause of those decisive reactions of our temperament towards an author's work which are so swift and unshakable; and they explain that admiration without liking which is the utmost we can give to some writers, and the liking without admiration we cannot help extending to others.

PENCILLINGS

If we judge this quality of soul, as we must, we are bound to judge it by moral standards. We pronounce instinctively, indeed; our reactions are immediate. We like, or do not like, the "atmosphere" of a book, just as we like, or do not like, the "atmosphere" of a person; and, in fact, we are judging a person through his book. No effort of his towards impersonality can deceive us. On the contrary, a true impersonality, involving, as it does, a closer correspondence between expression and apprehension than is achieved by the writer who permits himself—or a histrionic projection of himself—to appear, provides us with still more certain evidence of the quality of soul. We have, as it were, an essence, from which all superfluous matter has been removed; the last disguise is fallen

MORALITY AGAIN

from the writer's habits of thought and feeling. We may admire his skill and respect his literary ability, but if his quality of soul is mean, or trivial, or repellent, nothing can save him for us.

We may, or may not, call this judgment of ours moral; and certainly there is a sense in which it might with equal justice be called æsthetic, just as we speak knowingly of the beauty of a character, or say that the ideal of the human spirit is a harmony. But the comeliness for which we are looking is a moral comeliness; it is a quality of soul quite different from the quality of mind which manifests itself in the artistic perfection of a work of literature. And if we ought not, in the interest of clarity and truth, confuse the one with the other, equally we ought not imagine that one man

MORALITY AGAIN

can supply the other's place. We demand, and have the right to demand, both of them.

And not only is the moral judgment immediately involved in our consideration of any book worth considering at all; but when we pass from distinguishing between good books to pronouncing which are great ones, it is involved again. We require not merely a quality of soul, as we require a clear tone in a bell, but scope and comprehensiveness also. About this, too, Pater was in no doubt. "It is on the quality of the matter it informs and controls, its compass, its variety, its alliance to great ends, or the depth of the note of revolt, or the largeness of hope in it, that the greatness of literary art depends." Our judgment of greatness depends upon our sense that human destinies are squarely faced, that

MORALITY AGAIN

the author's soul was responsive to the deepest human doubts and bewilderments, and that his vision included the beauty and the joy and the ugliness and the sorrow of human life, glozing nothing. In the great work of literature we demand perfection of art, integrity of the writer's soul, and comprehensiveness in his attitude. Of these three qualities two are moral.

CLASSICAL TRANSLATIONS

THE new and beautiful edition of Samuel Butler's version of the *Odyssey* has raised the whole question of classical translations again. With a perceptible gleam in his eye Butler described his prose as having "the same benevolent inclination towards the Tottenham Court Road as Butcher and Lang's towards Wardour Street." That is said in the best Butler manner; it is the Parthian shot of a retiring man. But, in vexing the enemy, as often Butler hardly did justice to himself.

Butler's *Odyssey* is, in fact, a very fine prose translation, though it is not quite so fine as his *Iliad*, because it is more wilful.

CLASSICAL TRANSLATIONS

One ought to ask, I suppose, whether it is a perfect translation. But then I do not know what are the positive qualities of a perfect translation. The negative qualities are easier to settle. Poetry ought always to be rendered into prose. Since the aim of the translator should be to present his original as exactly as possible, no fetters of rhyme or metre must be imposed to hamper this difficult labour. Indeed, they make it impossible.

Of course, a poet is perfectly within his rights in striving to turn poetry into poetry. We should have lost one of Mr. Yeats's most exquisite poems if he had not been suffered to do his best with Ronsard's *Vieille Hélène*. And Sir Sidney Lee alone knows how many of the Elizabethan sonnets we so naively admire are really translations of Italian and French originals. But we are quite right in not worrying. The English poems exist, as they always have existed, in their own right. Nothing will prevent us from treating them as original work. So we regard some of Mr. Arthur Symons's beautiful versions from Verlaine. Chapman's *Homer* is likewise Chapman, even though Keats and Lamb believed it was something else.

And, it may be argued, Butler's *Odyssey* is Butler. It is indeed very much so, in one sense. It has a shrewd and almost pawky vividness that no other translation of Homer possesses. It is more precise than the *Odyssey* itself. We are conscious of Butler's personality as well as that of the author (or authoress) of the *Odyssey*. But so much of an alien element is necessary and desirable

CLASSICAL TRANSLATIONS

in a good translation. A translator must make his original real to himself, or his translation will be colourless. He strives to render exactly the value of each phrase as it appears to him. For another that value may be quite different. Some of us would find, for instance, that to write "rosy-fingered dawn" wherever that phrase appears in the *Odyssey* is to give the adjective an emphasis it does not really possess. Others would feel that to replace it occasionally by "rosy dawn" is little less than a sacrilege.

The medium in which the translator is working must exert its influence. Since prose is chosen as offering the least hindrance to exactness, it follows that discordant tones must be avoided. They will produce a sense of discrepancy which is quite foreign

PENCILLINGS

to the original. As Samuel Butler truly said, "Things are possible in poetry which are not possible in prose." For a proof of that simple statement look, for instance, at the opening lines of Andrew Lang's version of Theocritus:

"Sweet, meseems, is the whispering sound of yonder pine-tree, goatherd, that murmureth by the wells of water; and sweet are thy pipings."

The original is, we are told, artificial. But it is not artificial in that way. Whatever the secret of its composition may have been, to us its effect is simple.

"The whispering of the pine-tree there which murmurs by the springs is sweet, goatherd; and you pipe sweetly."

That is shorter. Surely, it is also better.

CLASSICAL TRANSLATIONS

The vice of the Wardour Street style of translation is that it is neither prose nor poetry. Instead of resolutely making up his mind that the musical element of the poetry must be sacrificed, the translator grasps desperately at "poetical" phrases. He corrupts his own prose without bringing us an inch nearer to the poetry of his original; and, by corrupting his own prose, he abandoned the chance of making real to us the underlying poetry of incident and atmosphere. Butler's *Odyssey* is Butler; but it is also the *Odyssey*. Butcher and Lang's *Odyssey* is not Butcher and Lang; neither is it the *Odyssey*. By that I mean that a man who is absolutely ignorant of the original will come much nearer to it by way of the Tottenham Court Road than he ever will by Wardour Street. Butler

PENCILLINGS

shows him the *Odyssey* through a coloured glass; Butcher and Lang interpose a frosted one.

And the Wardour Street translators have corrupted something more than their own prose; they have corrupted the youth of England. Year after year schoolboys and undergraduates repeat, with archaistic variations of their own, this degenerate "poetical" prose. A classical translation would not be a classical translation if it were not written in this jargon, which from its constant association with great names, gradually acquires the prestige of fine writing. And at length it is almost as difficult for a classical scholar to write a piece of hard, clean English as it is for a camel to pass through the eye of a needle. That is a minor misfortune, no doubt, and

CLASSICAL TRANSLATIONS

we can comfort ourselves with the thought that when the study of English becomes our only humanity it will pass away. But on that grim day the other evil will only be magnified. When we can read the classics only in "poetical" translations, we shall cease to read them at all.

We ought to begin to arm ourselves against that day. Butler has enriched us with a Homer that is a simple, vivid, and fascinating tale, through which unclassical generations will have at least a glimpse of the meaning of Greek clarity. Soon it will find its way into the nursery, and its immortality will be secure. But much besides Homer remains. The best thing would be that the modern poets and novelists should take hold of the business. The modern spirit, with its almost fanatical desire to get rid of the *poncif,* might make a fine thing of classical translation; and in the process it might learn the value of classical restraint.

My second thought, however, is that the modern writer seldom has any classics; and my third that he is too eager to be individual at all costs to be safely trusted with translating them. He is hardly modest enough to submit to the limitations imposed by the work. An extreme and patient honesty is quite as necessary as literary skill. Only in so far as he can reach a direct contact with his original will he be freed from the temptation to interpose either his own caprice or some acquired mannerism between it and the reader. Before he can make it real to others it must be real to him. The *Odyssey* was very real to Samuel Butler;

CLASSICAL TRANSLATIONS

so real that instead of making his darling Nausicaa wash raiment or garments or any of the things that nobody ever wears, he made her wash shirts. I fancy, too, that he liked to imagine they were his own shirts and that when he made her say " Papa, dear," she was talking to him. No wonder that his translation was thought improper.

DISRAELI ON LOVE

Mr. Walkley's recent praise of Disraeli as the novelist of love at first sight moved me, as it doubtless moved many others, to hunt out *Henrietta Temple*. Frankly, I was sceptical. Doubly sceptical, for there were two reasons for doubt. First, because love at first sight is a thing almost impossible for a writer to bring off. Hardly any one since Shakespeare has managed it convincingly, or succeeded in giving us the glamour without falling into extravagance. Even Lucy and Richard in *Richard Feverel* leave me, I confess, comparatively cold. Indeed, in my opinion the best modern attempt at love at first sight between grown-ups is contained in a page of Henry James's

DISRAELI ON LOVE

The Wings of the Dove, and between children in the first volume of Marcel Proust's incomparable and interminable narrative. The second reason was that Disraeli's flamboyant Corinthian manner seemed to me the least likely of all with which to achieve success.

My misgivings were justified. Not that I did not enjoy dipping into *Henrietta Temple.* I enjoyed it exceedingly. But not at all in the way I was intended, by Disraeli if not by Mr. Walkley, to enjoy it. The love-making between Ferdinand and Henrietta struck me as extraordinarily, irresistibly funny. Probably it was all up with Disraeli the moment he chose the name of Ferdinand. The lover of Miranda holds a place apart in the chronicles of love at first sight, and it must either be that Disraeli intended to emulate Shakespeare, which was rash in the extreme, or that he had forgotten Shakespeare, which was careless. Probably he had forgotten Shakespeare. Otherwise he would scarcely have dared to rephrase the sentiment, which Shakespeare himself did not dare to alter from the form the dead shepherd had given it: "Whoever loved, that loved not at first sight?" Disraeli wrote, as though it were a discovery of his own, "There is no love but love at first sight."

And just as that seems a dull version of Marlowe's line and Shakespeare's, Disraeli's lovers make a very poor (or a very rich) show. It is hard to believe in Henrietta at all. She had "a lofty and pellucid brow," at which for some reason I begin to smile; and the smile becomes a laugh when I read that "Language cannot describe the startling

DISRAELI ON LOVE

symmetry of her superb figure." But Henrietta, in any case, is a mere nothing compared to Ferdinand, "as, pale and trembling, he withdrew a few paces from the overwhelming spectacle and leant against a tree in a chaos of emotion." Can it be that modern lovers are a degenerate race? Or will the things that happen to them in books seem just as queer to our great-grandchildren as the things that happen to Ferdinand do to us. The poor man suffered terribly. "Silent he was, indeed, for he was speechless; though the big drop that quivered on his brow and the slight foam that played upon his lip proved the difficult triumph of passion over expression." That slight foam would terrify a modern Henrietta. Perhaps it would have frightened this one if she had been looking. Luckily, she was

PENCILLINGS

not. "She had gathered a flower and was examining its beauty."

However, Ferdinand pulled himself together when Henrietta's father, "of an appearance remarkably prepossessing," turned up. "Let me be your guide," said Ferdinand, advancing. Papa was decently grateful; but Henrietta was something more. "His beautiful companion rewarded Ferdinand with a smile like a sunbeam that played about her countenance"—how much nicer than the foam that had played about Ferdinand's!—"till it finally settled into two exquisite dimples, and revealed to him teeth that, for a moment, he believed to be even the most beautiful feature of that surpassing visage." Surpassing visage, like mobled queen, is good.

Certainly Ferdinand had enough to go

DISRAELI ON LOVE

on with. But more was to come. He was to discover that "from her lips stole forth a perfume sweeter than the whole conservatory." Surpassing lips! A little overpowering also. No wonder that "from the conservatory they stepped forth into the garden." There is nothing like a little fresh air. "The vespers of the birds were faintly dying away, the last low of the returning kine sounded over the lea, the tinkle of the sheep-bell was heard no more"—Disraeli knew his Gray better than his Shakespeare—"the thin white moon began to gleam, and Hesperus glittered in the faded sky. It was the twilight hour!" It was indeed, and Ferdinand played up to it like a man. Bending his head, he murmured to her: "Most beautiful, I love thee! . . . Beautiful, beloved Henrietta, I can

PENCILLINGS

no longer repress the emotions that since I first beheld you have vanquished my existence." And, to do him justice, he did not repress them. In fact, as Henry James would have said, he abounded in that sense. And Henrietta, though verbally less eloquent, rewarded him adequately.

For my part, I like it all immensely, but nothing could persuade me to take it seriously. Love at first sight is one thing, and that is another. Love at first sight is shy; Disraeli's account of it is like an explanation of a circus performance through a megaphone. " Amid the gloom and travail of existence suddenly to behold a beautiful being and as instantaneously to feel an overwhelming conviction that with that fair form for ever our destiny must be entwined. . . . " Jane Austen had read all about it when

DISRAELI ON LOVE

she wrote *Love and Freindship*. Laura felt the same about Talbot. "No sooner did I behold him first than I felt that on him the Happiness or Misery of my future life must depend." But Ferdinand is so extreme that Laura does not sound like a caricature beside him. On the contrary he makes her appear a completely rational being. Not to Laura's Edward, but to Henrietta's Ferdinand, ought his father have addressed the crushing question: "Where, Edward, in the name of wonder, did you pick up this unmeaning gibberish? You have been studying Novels, I suspect."

We also suspect that Disraeli had been "studying Novels" with a view to giving his public what it wanted hot and strong, just as he had studied the *Elegy in a Country Churchyard* in order to make his description

PENCILLINGS

of the twilight hour duly poetical. And his picture of love bears about as close a relation to any human reality as his paraphrase of the Elegy does to poetry. On any showing Disraeli was a remarkable man, but if he did not write the love scenes of *Henrietta Temple* with his tongue in his cheek—and I rather believe he did not—he was a far more remarkable man than the most enthusiastic Primrose Leaguer has ever imagined.

ORATORY AND LITERATURE

LAST week we allowed Disraeli to make fun of himself as the novelist of love. His exaggerated Corinthianism is an extreme case; it passes bodily over the narrow line that is said to divide the sublime from the ridiculous. It is, perhaps, more amusing than interesting, except as showing what a man may do and yet become Prime Minister of England. And yet, on second thoughts, may it not be that Disraeli's manner of writing actually helped him on his political career? I speak of his manner of writing only; there is matter enough in his novels, from *Sybil* onwards, to secure his reputation both as a political thinker and a political observer.

PENCILLINGS

Disraeli manages so to focus attention on himself that we easily forget that there were at least two other famous and popular writers in his day who had successful, though less eminent, political careers. Macaulay was one, Bulwer-Lytton the other. Lytton was almost as extravagantly Corinthian as Disraeli himself, and even Macaulay was slightly touched with the disease. It shows itself for brief moments in some of his finest pages. In the essay on Warren Hastings, for instance, he wrote of the trial, " There were gathered together from all parts of a great, free, enlightened and prosperous empire, grace and female loveliness, wit and learning, the representatives of every science and every art. . . . There appeared the voluptuous charms of her to whom the heir of the throne had in secret plighted his

ORATORY AND LITERATURE

faith." That is, of course, a mild outbreak compared to Disraeli's. In *Henrietta Temple* it would appear positively restrained. Nevertheless, it is Corinthian. "Female loveliness" and "voluptuous charms" are as characteristically Corinthian as "Surpassing visage" and "Transcendent form."

In the first part of Macaulay's sentence there is an audible echo of the periods of Mr. Pott of the *Eatanswill Gazette,* which suggests that the manner is primarily oratorical. It seems to have come naturally to the political writer of those days. From the oratorical to the rhetorical is a short step indeed. Originally they meant the same thing, and the modern distinction is hardly more than a nuance. We may say that rhetoric is oratory in the wrong place. A writer is rhetorical when he writes as though he were addressing a public meeting. For an orator to use vague, empty, resonant phrases is perfectly legitimate. His business is to produce an effect upon his audience; his skill, indeed, largely consists in not allowing them time to think whether there is any particular meaning in his sonorous periods. He knows that there is a vast difference between persuading a crowd and convincing an individual, and naturally he addresses himself solely to the task before him. That is why the speeches of famous orators generally make such intolerably dull reading. They were never meant to be read.

As Carlyle said, " The difference between speaking " (by which in his odd way he meant the utterance of the poet and the writer) " and public-speaking is altogether

ORATORY AND LITERATURE

generic. The meeting, by its very name, has environed itself in a given element of commonplace." And the orator has only "to keep on the soft, safe, parallel course; parallel to the Truth or nearly so; for Heaven's sake not in contact with it: no obstacle will meet him; on the favouring given element of commonplace he triumphantly careers." Carlyle was severe; but was he unfair? The vague impressiveness which is a virtue of oratory—ninety years ago, it is worth noting, Carlyle picked out as specimen *clichés* of the orator, " The rights of suffering millions," and " the divine gift of song," which are still worked hard to-day —is one of the worst of vices in writing. It absolutely prevents that precise symbolical rendering of thought and vision in which literature consists. You cannot swallow a

PENCILLINGS

good piece of literature like a bolus; it needs attention, careful savouring, slow degustation. The orator's audience has no time for that. It cannot pause over his sentences. They roll steadily on. Unless they were mainly commonplace, they would not be understood.

There is plenty of excuse for the orator; but oratory is not literature. Lincoln's "Gettysburg Address" was laboriously made literature before it was spoken, and remained literature afterward. Cicero and Demosthenes, I imagine, carried their speeches home to their studies and turned them into literature. And the two most magnificent speeches in the world were invented by writers to take the place of those actually delivered. Plato composed Socrates's immortal Apology, and Thucydides wrote

ORATORY AND LITERATURE

Pericles's funeral oration; they are no more orations in the true sense than Othello's "And say besides that in Aleppo once——" Imaginary speeches are in the nature of things better than real ones, which are not meant to survive the moment of utterance save in the painful pages of *Hansard*. If they are preserved elsewhere than in that repertory of *cliché* and incoherence, they reveal themselves for what they are, pale ghosts of a true human utterance. Look, for instance, at the closing sentences of Burke's speech, which Macaulay is rash enough to quote. "Therefore hath it with all confidence been ordered, by the Commons of Great Britain and Ireland, that I impeach Warren Hastings of high crimes and misdemeanours. I impeach him in the name of the Commons' House of Parliament, whose trust he has betrayed. I impeach him in the name of the English nation, whose ancient honour he has sullied. I impeach him in the name of the people of India, whose rights he has trodden underfoot, and whose country he has turned into a desert. Lastly, in the name of human nature itself, in the name of both sexes, in the name of every age, in the name of every rank, I impeach the common enemy and oppressor of all."

It is hardly credible—until we remember what unspeakable trash were the words of the speeches with which Mrs. Siddons played upon her audiences—that the audience was moved to tears by this vain repetition. Macaulay would have been kinder to Burke's reputation if he had invented a speech for him.

ORATORY AND LITERATURE

The orator-writer is in a difficult case. Either he carries over his oratory into his writing, which then becomes emptily rhetorical; or he carries over his writing into his oratory, which then becomes obscure and incomprehensible. Both Disraeli and Lytton, we may fairly say, carried the platform manner into their books. Macaulay was more successful in keeping a distinction between them. There is a touch of rhetoric in his writing, but on the whole it does not affect his substance; it is apparent rather in the movement and tempo. His writing has the swift and monotonous rhythm of vigorous speech. Nevertheless, it is writing and not oratory, though sometimes it seems to hover perilously between. Perhaps we can describe its quality by saying that it is the style of a public man, though not of a public speaker. It is not a style for which we can feel any intimate affection; but we must admire its indubitable magnificence.

In distinguishing between oratory and literature, we touch the fringe of another question which it is impossible to explore and timorous to leave aside. What is the relation between the language of drama and the language of oratory? The answer seems to be that generally the language of drama is oratory and occasionally literature. *Henry V.* is mainly oratory, and that is why it holds the stage, although it is very poor Shakespeare and very poor drama. Mr. Drinkwater's *Abraham Lincoln* is decidedly oratorical, though in a different way. But Shakespeare is, on the whole, so seldom oratorical that it is a perpetual wonder to

ORATORY AND LITERATURE

me how his audiences managed to understand many of the speeches in his plays at a first hearing. We, who have the book, and know most of them (if only vaguely) by heart, find that our closest attention is necessary. How on earth the base mechanical managed to find his way about in them I cannot imagine. Perhaps he did not even try, but waited complacently and confidently for the final murders.

ON UNPLEASANT CHARACTERS

WE were talking about novels. "I suppose literary critics," said my companion, "don't care twopence whether a novel depresses them or not." Trying at a venture to distinguish, I replied that I thought that they didn't like to be depressed any more than other people, but perhaps they were not always depressed by precisely the same things. I was going to develop the argument when my companion interposed. "I don't mind deaths or murders," he said, laughing. His laughter is so complete and contagious that I felt that deaths and murders were the happiest little accidents. "But I can't stand unpleasant characters," he added.

UNPLEASANT CHARACTERS

And suddenly I found that I had no reply. I could not remember whether I could stand unpleasant characters or not.

I went upstairs to think it over; and the more I thought the less could I remember any unpleasant characters in fiction at all. Whenever I seemed to have my finger on one and began to scrutinise him, or what I remembered of him, he changed into something odd, or fantastic, or amusing. I began at the beginning with that nominally most undesirable character, Chaucer's Pandarus, who is reputed to have been the first member of his scandalous profession. Yet, in retrospect at least, Pandarus seems delightful. He wants the two people he loves to be happy and damn the consequences.

PENCILLINGS

> " Though all this town cried on this thing by note
> I nolde sette at that noise a grote."

He doesn't think much of men in general: a pack of noisy, silly sheep. All the more reason then why the nice people should have a good time. It is impossible even to call him a cynic, for there is not a touch of contempt in his worldly wisdom, but there is a great deal of tenderness. Pandarus is, in fact, the kindly but unsentimental uncle to perfection, and I can't help thinking that he is the nearest thing we have to a portrait of Chaucer himself.

Chaucer was evidently no good. I passed on to Shakespeare. All his disreputable characters are enchanting, even down to Lucio in *Measure for Measure;* as to his

UNPLEASANT CHARACTERS

villains, male and female, "unpleasant" is the last epithet one would dream of applying to them. Iago, Goneril, Regan —one does not even hate them; they are much too big, much too—how shall we say it?—elemental to be hated. And something like this happens with all the members of the Squeers family. They are transformed; they cease to be repulsive; they are, to use a transcendental metaphor, uplifted into the world of essences. The moment Mr. Squeers, smacking his lips over the twopennyworth of blue milk in the half-gallon of water, has declared, "There's richness for you," he himself becomes too rich to be unpleasant any more. Becky Sharp and Lord Steyne would, I suppose, be very unpleasant customers to meet in real life; in *Vanity Fair* they worry us not at all. And

PENCILLINGS

Rodolphe in *Madame Bovary,* who perhaps comes nearest to what we should ordinarily describe as an unpleasant man, whose very moustaches are an offence, has in recollection a perfect right to his own existence. Then there is cockney Huish in *The Ebb Tide*; but Stevenson, being an incorrigible romantic, made him as brave as the devil at the last.

As you see, I enjoyed myself greatly in hunting up these old companions. There were dozens more of them, but to my purpose nothing. And yet in the contemporary novels that I read, I find unpleasant characters in plenty. I will not mention them by name, partly for fear of offending, partly for reasons which will subsequently appear. For the question I set myself to answer was: What is the cause of the difference? The

UNPLEASANT CHARACTERS

pessimist would have a short way with it and declare that writers nowadays are but shadows of their forefathers.

I do not believe it. There is plenty of good writing being done in 1922, and some of it is good in new ways. And if the kind of society that is often pictured in modern novels seems rather more sordid than it was in novels of fifty or a hundred years ago, I do not know that sordidness is in itself much worse than silliness.

I fancy the answer to the question is less depressing, though perhaps (at least in its implications) not quite so simple. The root of the matter seems to be that we do not remember really unpleasant characters. We forget them, not because of that admirably human habit of passing the sponge over things we do not care to remember, but

PENCILLINGS

simply because an unpleasant character who is unpleasantly presented has no claim upon our memory. It is the manner of presentation which is vital. If the writer presents his unpleasant character creatively, that is with (among other things) a sense of his individuality as one of the creatures of the various universe, the character is transfigured. If the writer has what we may call the disinterestedness of pure creation, the unpleasantness is dissolved away in the vivid light of art. The characters which have suffered this sea-change, " of whose bones are coral made," are the only unpleasant characters we remember, because they are the only ones which compel us to remember them.

Naturally, there are more unpleasant characters in modern fiction than in the

UNPLEASANT CHARACTERS

literature we remember. We remember only the immortals, whereas modern books are only the raw material of immortality; they contain unpleasant characters, unpleasantly presented, whom we shall forget, either because their authors have no creative power at all, or because, having creative power, they have turned it to base uses and have abandoned disinterestedness to satisfy some grudge they have conceived against life or humanity. Those who have the habit of reading know the feeling when in even the cleverest of books they are repelled by an almost inaudible undertone of snarling and resentment. In a word, in a phrase, that is ugly, irredeemably ugly in itself, they see *le bout de l'oreille qui perce,* and sometimes have a glimpse of much more than the tip of the ear, of a whole row of bared and angry fangs.

Unpleasantness is an ambiguous attribute. All Shakespeare's "irregular humorists"—blessed name for Bardolph, Nym, and Pistol—would have been unpleasant enough in life; so, as Charles Lamb admitted, would many of Congreve's characters: but in the world of literature they are wonderful. Unpleasant in life, they are pleasant, much more than pleasant, in books, because the minds of their creators worked serenely free of quotidian limitation. But in Wycherly, and still more in Smollett, and surely also in Swift's picture of the Yahoos, we catch the hateful hiss of an exasperation beyond control. Their unpleasant characters *are* unpleasant. What we have to do is to avoid confusing what is unpleasant in life

UNPLEASANT CHARACTERS

with what is unpleasant in literature. It is not so difficult as it sounds, for creative integrity is much easier to discern than to define.

DR. JOHNSON AND THE SWALLOWS

This morning I watched the swallows wheeling against a sky of that faded blue which tells of a glorious summer day to come. When they glided beneath the sun their wings became suddenly transparent, the plumage seemed burned away in a golden fire. Had I not been a slave of the inkpot the sight of them would have more than sufficed me; I should have followed their interwoven paths through the trackless air, until the pure beauty of their motion made my eyes dizzy; I should have saturated myself with the vision of a perfect thing.

But, alas, I am what I am, and that

DR. JOHNSON AND THE SWALLOWS

is something worse than Anton Tchehov's Trigorin, whose soul was so pickled in ink that he could not look at a cloud without putting down in his mental notebook that it was like a piano, or a weasel, or a whale. That served at all events to fix the cloud for ever in his mind, whereas I, looking at the swallows, said to myself " Dr. Johnson," who was not in the least like a swallow.

I waited a moment for my dilatory mind to give some reason for its astonishing behaviour. Why had the waves of the unconscious thrown up that name, that image rather, of all others on the shore of my attention?

I was bewildered. One of the detached, observant egos that attend us watched curiously a man whose bodily eye was fixed upon the wheeling swallows while his inward eye gazed with a puzzled admiration upon the gray wig and brown greatcoat of the Doctor. What could *he* be doing there?

The swallows still circled unwearied round about the sun. Perhaps I was bemused by them; for it did not occur to me to wonder whether Dr. Johnson had spoken some wise words about swallows. It was the presence of his image I had to explain. And in a little while I remembered that my companion had criticised, some hours before, a common friend for biting his nails, and I, in an impulse of charity, had been on the point of saying, "But Dr. Johnson also bit his nails." I did not actually say it, because my companion carries reverence for Dr. Johnson to such a point that I should have gained opprobrium for myself and

DR. JOHNSON AND THE SWALLOWS

nothing for our friend by doing so. Indeed his vice would have been aggravated by the reminder that Dr. Johnson shared it.

Dr. Johnson had been suppressed therefore. Now he had bobbed up at the first opportunity. That was settled. But why were swallows an opportunity for him? Again I watched them with half-closed eyes. "Swallows? Dr. Johnson?" I questioned silently. I repeated the incantation and waited. At last, out of I know not what store of forgotten memories, came the answer. "A number of them conglobulate together by flying round and round, and they sleep through the winter at the bottom of a stream." It must, I suppose, be somewhere in Boswell, or can it be in the Dictionary? There, at any rate, the swallows

PENCILLINGS

were, flying round and round, perhaps in the very act of *conglobulation*.

And yet, a moment since, before I had begun to watch them, I should have been positive that Dr. Johnson had never said a word about swallows. The only reason I can suggest for the emergence of the forgotten memory is the one I have suggested; that Dr. Johnson had been suppressed and had seized the first opening to reappear. There, at any rate, he also was, with his bitten nails and his shoes with no right and left, substantially before me, offering me the oddest of odd words to describe the serene orbits of the swallows about the sun. Moreover, he would not go away. There was something more about him that I had to remember.

Yes, somewhere I had lately seen a new

DR. JOHNSON AND THE SWALLOWS

fact about him—something that clamoured to be added to my slender store, another touch of colour for that picture of the childlike tyrant which each of us carries somewhere in his mind. What was it? Where had I seen it? Again, I slowly began to remember. It was in a *Literary Supplement*. But which? And had I got it? I must go and see. "Don't go now," cried the swallows. "We are more important than Dr. Johnson." And one of them, to prove it, plunged clean into the sun, flamed into nothing, was reborn like the phœnix, and scattered gold from his new-fledged wings.

But the slave of the inkpot has his ears stopped with wax against such siren voices. He turned away from the swallows to rummage among old newspapers, and for

PENCILLINGS

once his virtue was rewarded. In Johnson's Dictionary, wrote the unknown reviewer, "The verb 'sip' is followed by the explanation: '1, To drink in small draughts; to take, at one apposition of the mouth, no more than the mouth will contain.' The Oxford Dictionary supplies nothing which justifies this maximum usage of the mouth in a 'sip,' and we fancy it is due to the influence of the quotation immediately following:—

> 'And sip with nymphs their elemental tea.'"

We know what Dr. Johnson did when he drank his twenty cups of tea; it is pleasant to know also that he believed he was sipping it.

Could it be, I finally wondered, that the swallows had been the hidden cause of this

DR. JOHNSON AND THE SWALLOWS

recollection, too, not only indirectly but directly also? For instance: Swallows sip indeed, while Dr. Johnson sipped only in his own imagination. Or perhaps: where others sip, Dr. Johnson swallows. That seems rather far-fetched; but associations are very far-fetched things. We track them down finally in the remotest corners of the mental world. Of all journeys of discovery none are more romantic or more thrilling than those we make in pursuit of them; and as in all the best journeys the return is even more exciting than the outward passage. Unlike terrestrial voyages, these of the mind are easy. There are no passport difficulties; we travel like princes or prime ministers; and there is always a sleeper to be had for the asking at the end of a train of thought.

SERIOUSNESS

It is becoming a habit with modern critics to talk much of artistic "seriousness." Matthew Arnold set the fashion originally, and he picked it up from Aristotle. Arnold admirably translated "spoudaiotês" as "high seriousness," and since then seriousness has become one of the shibboleths of serious criticism. I am myself no small offender. I am continually demanding seriousness. But my conscience has begun to prick me, and I have begun to wonder what it means.

I imagine that when we say a writer is serious, we mean that he has a morality, that he is communicating to us the

SERIOUSNESS

profoundest truth that he feels about human life. This truth of the writer cannot be formulated as an intellectual judgment; is an intuitional, emotional, qualitative certainty, which cannot be summed up in a verdict, but only communicated through a work of literature. In other words a serious piece of literature is one which has validity. It illuminates our human experience. It puts us in a position whence a clear view of human life is possible. When we have read *Don Quixote* we seem to see the double thread of ideal and actual that is entwined in all human action. We receive a like vision from *Le Misanthrope;* we see the hopelessness of demanding that human beings should be ideal.

That these two works immediately suggest

PENCILLINGS

themselves as examples of seriousness in literature shows plainly that fine comedy is just as serious as fine tragedy. Instinctively we know that is true, and yet the ordinary implications of the word serious seem to prevent us from realising it. At least I can see no other way of accounting for a curious " might have been " in that stimulating volume, *The Sacred Wood.* " How astonishing," Mr. Eliot wrote in it, " if Arnold had shown his contemporaries exactly *why* the author of *Amos Barton* was a more serious writer than Dickens, and *why* the author of *La Chartreuse de Parme* is more serious than either." Astonishing indeed! is the immediate reply, —astonishing as any other murder of impossibility. But Mr. Eliot, though he noticeably refrains from telling us " exactly

SERIOUSNESS

why," most evidently does believe that George Eliot is a more serious writer than Dickens. And that is odd. One can only suggest that the word serious has proved a pitfall for Mr. Eliot's careful feet, and that he has come to believe that George Eliot was a more serious writer than Dickens, because his creation was mainly comic, while hers was mainly tragic.

One suspects also the influence of another word-suggestion; namely that the writer is pre-eminently serious who takes himself seriously. George Eliot, under Lewes's inspiration, came to take herself seriously indeed, and the result was *Romola,* in fact disastrous. Doubly disastrous, because *Romola* is as dead as *Salammbô,* and because (as her husband said) she began it a young woman and finished it an old one.

PENCILLINGS

George Eliot was a great writer, but she was born with enough seriousness to last her a lifetime. Her chief need was to keep herself unbent, instead of making herself taut and old in the effort to achieve a serious masterpiece. And, great writer as she is, she is a small one beside Dickens. So for the matter of that is Stendhal, and Dickens is, in any valuable critical sense of the word, more serious than either. His comic vision was the fiercest that has ever been in English literature, so savage as to be sometimes all but unbearable. What could be more terrifying than the final quarrel between Sarah Gamp and Betsy Prig? Dickens probably roared with laughter when he wrote it, we do when we read it; but if we happen to stop laughing and get a clear sight of

SERIOUSNESS

what he is showing us, we do not laugh again.

Seriousness, yes. It is the vital quality of enduring literature. But for heaven's sake let us not begin to confuse it with tragedy or solemnness. When Mr. Wells wrote *Mr. Polly,* he was a serious writer, though he laughed all the while; when he wrote *The Secret Places of the Heart,* he was not, though he pulled a long face over it. Seriousness comes from a keen vision of life and a deep feeling about it. And that is not altered by laughter or tears. Great comedy is terrible; we laugh at it, it sometimes seems, only to prevent ourselves from seeing it, and when we do see it we flinch as we never do from tragedy, because it is more sudden and more cruel.

PENCILLINGS

There is yet another alien nuance to be traced in this word seriousness. It is often ascribed to the work of a writer who is very serious about the technique of his craft. Dickens is sometimes a careless writer, more careless of the build of his sentences than George Eliot, though hardly more careless than Stendhal. In this sense Flaubert is *the* serious writer. But though we may freely admit that it is a good thing to be serious in Flaubert's way, we must also admit that it is incompatible with a great creative energy. A man from whose brain Squeers is pushing out Micawber and Pecksniff being jostled by Podsnap cannot spend years over a single book, or days over a single page; he simply hasn't the time. This kind of seriousness is a minor virtue, but no amount of

SERIOUSNESS

it will replace the seriousness that is vital.

We must not confuse it, neither must we despise it. We may legitimately share the contempt of a famous novelist for " holiday authors," for the men " Who sit down to write a book as they would sit down to a game of cards—leisurely—living people who coolly select as an amusement to kill time, an occupation which can only be pursued, even creditably, by the patient, uncompromising reverent devotion of every intelligent faculty, more or less, which a human being has to give." Noble words! And the novelist who wrote them was not Flaubert, nor George Eliot, nor Stendhal, nor Balzac, nor Dickens, nor Hardy—but Wilkie Collins. What shall we say then? Beware of seriousness? Probably that is

PENCILLINGS

safer advice than " Be serious!" For the seriousness that matters cannot be won by pains; while the seriousnesses that do not matter may lead to *The Moonstone* and perhaps to *The Law and the Lady.*

THE COURAGE OF CRITICISM

ONE of the hardest things for a critic to do is to present an unbiassed mind to a new book. That is the critic's private concern, some may say, shying instantly at the unpopular word, and he were best to keep it to himself. But criticism is not a highly specialised profession like medicine or the law. Every reader is a potential critic, and in so far as he reads well an actual one. Some people try to communicate and impose their critical opinions—a pursuit which is a branch of the art of literature; these are the professional critics—if you like, the critic *par excellence*. But it is not because they are critics that they are a race apart, but because they are or try to be artists; just as artists in the larger sense have perceptions of the same kind as those of other people, and are distinguished only by the will and power to communicate them. So that when we say that nothing is harder for the critic than to present an unbiassed mind to a new book, we are not airing a professional hardship but a general disability.

The difficulty is most sensible when we come to the onerous and delightful act of passing judgment. Onerous, because in the act of judgment we are ourselves judged; delightful, because the majority of new books are not worth judging at all, and the act of judgment is the pinnacle of a rare enjoyment which is incomplete without it. By failing to judge we " blunt the fine point

THE COURAGE OF CRITICISM

of seldom pleasure." A book has made a vivid impression on our minds. We lean back in our chair and say to ourselves, " Now, *how* good is it really? " We have a suspicion that we may have been taken in. We are reluctant to trust ourselves, and instinctively we reach out for the staff of authority to lean upon. We obey Arnold's precept and conjure up fragments of the writings that are immortal. Alas, they give no help. The new thing is not like them, simply because it is new.

Our instinct is to hedge. Yes, we say, the book made a vivid impression, but how crude is the writing! The visions are definite, but may not that be because they are soulless? Or, contrariwise, we say of a book that has appeared to us misty and stale and flat. But how beautifully *written*!

PENCILLINGS

The dull haze in which the characters are hidden we liken to the cloud in which the loving gods wrapped the Homeric hero; it is poetic, imaginative. In either case we are seeking in the past for a buttress to our present insecurity. The writing of the misty book is like the writing we have learned to admire; the writing of the vivid book is quite unlike it. It is not decorous and polished, it is not plaintive and musical. It makes us, now that we have escaped from its spell, vaguely uncomfortable that it should so have moved us. Perhaps—can it be—God forbid—that we are lacking in taste?

If you have the instinct for such discriminations you can pick up the trail of this uncertainty all through contemporary criticism. You will find the reviewer who

THE COURAGE OF CRITICISM

has evidently been moved by a book shrinking away from it. Yes, it was vivid, he admits, but lacking in imagination. As though a book really could be vivid without imagination! What he is really lamenting is the absence of poeticisation, of what is called "imaginative writing." He cannot get rid of the sneaking feeling that it is wrong to admire a book that does not contain it. To cast a vivid light on to reality, without mitigating mists, seems to him in spite of himself, almost cruel, even a little vulgar. But when he finds his imaginative writing again he is comfortable; he feels the presence of "art," and he is happier or he pretends to be.

This might be called artistic snobbery, and it is truly a kind of snobbery in that the critic has not the courage to judge the

PENCILLINGS

book in and for itself. He is like a man in a railway carriage who, when an acquaintance enters, breaks off an interesting conversation with a shabby-looking fellow because he is afraid of the uplifted eyebrow. He cannot trust himself. Another manifestation of this same snobbery is the half-convinced ecstacy of praise which bursts forth when a book appears in the raiment of "poetry." It is a pretty safe rule to mistrust a review of any novel in which great emphasis is laid upon its poetic character.

I resist the temptation to digress on to the question of how to read reviews, and repeat that truly imaginative writing seldom reads like it. Our concept of imaginative writing is a composite picture of all the styles which have at one time or another

THE COURAGE OF CRITICISM

been given that name; and it is obviously impossible for a piece of good writing to correspond with that. And this is one of the reasons why some of the more original writers to-day never receive their fair share of critical attention. Superficially they do not look like literary artists, as, for instance, Mr. W. W. Jacobs does not. But Mr. Jacobs has created a world, a little world it is true, but a world of his own. He is a much more important figure in literature than a dozen younger writers whose works are always received with respectful attention. But Mr. Jacobs is comic and popular: *snobisme oblige.* How can serious criticism deal with a figure like the Night Watchman? And there are so many cases like his, of writers who do their business unobtrusively, without pretension, who never air their

PENCILLINGS

views on literature at large or the future of the novel, and for their modesty are never taken into consideration, that at times we have the unpleasant feeling that a hundred years hence criticism may appear to have been as wide of the mark as the critics of a hundred years ago to us now.

Perhaps it all comes to this: that we are too conscientious, too Puritan. We can with difficulty persuade ourselves that a book we enjoy can really be a good one. So flowery a path should lead not to happiness but to the everlasting bonfire. And yet, good heavens, how enjoyable good literature is! When we look back it is the sense and memory of delight, golden delight, which most potently remains. Does any one forget when he first plunged away from the familiar paths in Chaucer and

THE COURAGE OF CRITICISM

entered on *Troilus and Cressida*? What a divine draught was that! And *Much Ado* and *Comus* and *Emma*! Every masterpiece is a fountain of sheer delight, grave delight in the *Purgatorio* and *King Lear*, gay delight in *Don Quixote* and *Henry IV.*, but for ever delight. So it has always been; it must be so still.

ON READING REVIEWS

IN the palmy days of literary journalism in the 'thirties and 'forties, when there were many literary papers, some of them were written practically from cover to cover by the editor's unaided hand. He managed to get through his work by quoting literally. Sometimes he would go on reviewing the same book for a month, sandwiching a few lines of his own text between columns and columns of the original. If he was a page or two short he would send down to the printer a marked copy of one of the books on his table and tell him to fill up with that. Leigh Hunt was an expert at the game.

ON READING REVIEWS

Those times are over, and yet it is possible to regret their passing. For nothing will give us so exact an idea of the quality of a book as a good substantial piece of the original text chosen as characteristic by some one who knows his business. No amount of descriptive epithets, of critical praise or blame will serve half so well as that. We have the matter for judgment before us, and we are free to form our own conclusions. And it is interesting to compare these conclusions of ours with those which the reviewer advances as his own. When we disagree with him, as we pretty often do, we are nevertheless grateful to him for his honesty. He seems to put his cards on the table and to be saying in the friendliest way: "That's my opinion. What's yours?"

PENCILLINGS

Yet these excellent reviews with generous quotation sometimes fill us with a kind of despair. "Mr. Spettigue," says the enthusiast, "has the authentic gift of poetry," and to prove it he quotes a couple of verses from which the authentic gift seems conspicuously absent. If that is poetry, we say to ourselves, then we must begin our education all over again. We are at loggerheads with the reviewer, there is no hope of our being reconciled on this side of eternity. And that is depressing. For although it is foolish to hope for a consensus of opinion on questions of literary taste, we desire it nevertheless, and we are distressed to discover that a man of evident goodwill holds on such a matter a conviction clean contrary to our own.

There is a particular interest in any review

ON READING REVIEWS

that mentions the word "genius" and backs it up with a quotation. We are always on the look-out for some one who will tell us what literary genius is, who will put his finger on a passage of a modern writer—we know all about the old ones—and say, "This is it." For genius is a distinctly romantic word; it seems to imply something over and above original talent or individual style, it carries vague but impressive associations of guardian spirits and affable, familiar ghosts, and also of Mr. Mortimer Knag, "who took to scorning everything and became a genius." There is something irremediably Byronic and Bohemian about the word. A genius is, we feel, a queer creature who is not very careful about his shirt, and there is something queer about his writing as well. It is unexpected and

PENCILLINGS

incalculable. All the more reason then why we should welcome any attempt to make our notion of the thing more definite.

Accordingly I prick up my ears whenever the word "genius" is applied to a writer to whom I have never heard it applied before, and I become all attention when the award is accompanied, as it always should be, by some indication of what is meant by genius, or better still, by a quotation which is evidence of it. The other day it was unflinchingly applied to the final verse of Mr. Masefield's *The Window in The Bye-Street.*

"Dully they watch her, then they turn to go
To that high Shropshire upland of late hay;

ON READING REVIEWS

> Her singing lingers with them as they mow,
> And many times they try it, now grave, now gay,
> Till with full throat over the hills away
> They lift it clear; oh, very clear it towers,
> Mixed with the swish of many falling flowers."

"That," said the reviewer, "is genius." I admired his courage and disagreed with his judgment. Mr. Masefield may or may not be a genius; very likely he is; certainly he has that curious inequality which is often associated with the name. The point is not whether Mr. Masefield has genius, but whether that particular verse has. I cannot see it, and if I were really pressed, I should have to confess that the last line and a half seem to me really bad.

PENCILLINGS

I remember another review, of a novel by a woman which created some stir a little while ago. The review ended with : " Hats off, gentlemen, a genius! " This time there was unfortunately no quotation, but its place was to some extent supplied by the reviewer's explanation why he said of her what Schumann said of Chopin: " She infuses her people and their surroundings with a poetic energy, an imaginative radiance which, outside poetry, is only to be met with in the works of such novelists as Dostoevsky." Immediately, I began to suspect that the reviewer had been taken in, that the novel with which he was so enchanted was full of vague poeticalities, that it took place nowhere in particular, and the characters were nothing very definite. And the odd phrase, " such novelists as

ON READING REVIEWS

Dostoevsky," made suspicion a certainty. There are no such novelists as Dostoevsky, there are no such novelists as Dickens, there are no such dramatists as Shakespeare. They are independent and incommensurable.

Reading reviews is a minor and fascinating science like the study of the continental Bradshaw. The most satisfying reviews are those which back up their judgments with quotations, for then we have the delight of agreeing or the distress of disagreeing *en connaissance de cause*. But in a review without quotations we can often find enough clues to the writer's attitude to enable us to decide whether we are likely to agree with his verdict. In these days when the books are multiplied as greatly as the literary papers are diminished, and

PENCILLINGS

liberal quotation is rarely possible, we need to cultivate, if only for our own amusement, the faculty of reading between the lines.

CONGREVE AND MOLIÈRE

FASHION in reading, as in all things else, is fickle. Ibsen is not read nowadays half so much as he was fifteen or twenty years ago when earnest young men cut their wisdom teeth on *Hedda Gabler* and *The Master-Builder*. For some reason he is now become almost as dowdy as the suburban society which he depicted in his plays. And this year the Molière tercentenary came to remind us that the great French dramatist is not so much regarded as he was. There were a dozen perfunctory articles and one good one; conscience-stricken people said "they must read Molière again" in an unconvincing, parenthetical way which

PENCILLINGS

suggested that they had not read him once; and the big sleeping dog was let lie. An older generation which had Molière at its finger-ends has been succeeded by one which has barely touched him with its finger-tips.

It was not, therefore, altogether surprising to find one of the leaders of the moderns, Mr. Clive Bell, lately declaring in his provocative way: "Yes: I put Congreve above Molière." Whether the challenge has been taken up I do not know. It is, perhaps, a statement to which the older generation would not deign, and the younger would not care, to reply. Nevertheless, it would be a pity if in this year of nominal piety to the master of comedy a judgment so uncompromising were allowed to go by default.

CONGREVE AND MOLIÈRE

Mr. Clive Bell, who does not fire off his thunderbolts unadvisedly, gives two reasons for his verdict. First, Molière's attitude to life " reminds him too often of the attitude of *Punch* "—not the famous figure of Guignol, I imagine, but our own comic weekly—and he thinks that

" ' La parfaite raison fuit toute extremité
 Et veut que l'on soit sage avec sobriété.'

really means, in the long run, that the *bourgeoisie* knows best." It would need a very long run indeed: but of that later. The second argument is an argument from style. "Molière wrote perfectly adequate French verse, whereas Congreve wrote prose which is always dazzlingly brilliant and sometimes exquisite." No one would dispute the description of Congreve's prose,

PENCILLINGS

or deny that Molière's verse *is* perfectly adequate. But whereas Molière's verse is always adequate, it is very doubtful whether Congreve's prose is. Is not the chief reason why *The Way of the World* has always failed on the stage the excessive brilliance of a dialogue which obscures the action and does not allow us to see the wood for the trees? And when it comes to comparing two comic dramatists, surely the fact that Molière is infinitely the better dramatist should count for something. His plays are as actor-proof as Shakespeare's.

The antithesis, moreover, between the adequacy of Molière's verse and the exquisiteness of Congreve's prose is meant to imply that Molière's verse was never exquisite. That is an odd idea. Take, for

CONGREVE AND MOLIÈRE

a single instance, Agnès's speech in *L'École des Femmes*:

" J'étois sur le balcon à travailler au frais
 Lorsque je vis passer sous les arbres d'auprès
 Un jeune homme bien fait, qui rencontrant ma vue,
 D'une humble révérence aussitôt me salue :
 Moi, pour ne point manquer à la civilité,
 Je fis la révérence aussitôt de mon côté.
Soudain il me refait une autre révérence :
 Moi, j'en refais de même une autre en diligence ;
 Et lui d'une troisième aussitôt repartant,
 D'une troisième aussi j'y repars à l'instant.

PENCILLINGS

Il passe, vient, repasse, et toujours de plus belle
Me fait à chaque fois révérence nouvelle ;
Et moi, qui tous ces tours fixement regardois,
Nouvelle révérence aussi je lui rendois:
Tant que, si sur ce point la nuit ne fût venue,
Toujours comme cela je me serois tenue,
Ne voulant point céder, et recevoir l'ennui
Qu'il me pût estimer moins civile que lui."

If that is not exquisite verse, I do not know the meaning of the phrase. The real difference between Molière and Congreve in this particular matter is that Molière's verse is always exquisite when exquisiteness

CONGREVE AND MOLIÈRE

is necessary, while Congreve's prose is often exquisite when something more straightforward would serve his purposes better. Millamant is wonderful and speaks divinely: but Agnès is just as wonderful, she speaks just as divinely, and she is as firm in outline and as clear as a crystal.

L'École des Femmes, for all its purity and completeness, is but a minor comedy of Molière's, yet it is equal to anything of Congreve's. With *Le Misanthrope* or *Tartuffe* we pass into a realm of profound comic reality which Congreve with all his genius could not enter. Put the equation grossly: Celimène is at least the equivalent of Millamant, and what has Congreve to show for Alceste? Congreve's graceful yacht is dwarfed by the side of Molière's splendid schooner. Congreve's draught, his weight, his substance is smaller, and so is his beauty. *Le Misanthrope* is one of the most perfect things in all literature: it is also one of the most substantial. To pit Congreve's exquisiteness against Molière's adequacy is to make a false antithesis and to mistake the accidents for the essentials of style.

But strangest of all is the paradoxical opinion that Molière's attitude, " in the long run," meant that the *bourgeoisie* knows best. Since when has harmony of the faculties been a bourgeois virtue? Does the bourgeois Arnolphe (de la Source), to take *L'École des Femmes* again, know best? Is Orgon infallible, or Georges Dandin the fountain of mundane wisdom? No doubt, Molière did not possess the common element which Mr. Bell so curiously finds in Flaubert

CONGREVE AND MOLIÈRE

and Machiavelli, and no less curiously calls their " fine intellectuality." He had something better, a point of view which would have enabled him to see the comic side of Flaubert's anti-bourgeois *emportement,* and to savour the aridity of Machiavelli's intellectualism. Molière may not have been an intellectual, but he was reasonable, and that is a much more difficult thing to be. Harmonious rationality is not generally supposed to be a bourgeois attribute, and certainly Molière did not represent it as one: it is more often ascribed to Greek civilisation in its brief maturity. To call Molière's attitude bourgeois beside Congreve's is not to criticise Molière, but Congreve himself. Molière is central, Congreve is eccentric. Molière's light is steady, Congreve's, with all its dazzling

PENCILLINGS

brilliance, flickers. Molière's vision is searching, Congreve's is superficial. We read Congreve for his verbal wit and the delicate beauty of one splendid scene, we read Molière for his wisdom and his truth, and it is only when he is challenged that we worry to point out the high and exquisite perfection of his art.

FACT AND FICTION

A CORRESPONDENT, who is a doctor, has written to me to ask me why, in a recent article, I called *Don Quixote* a masterpiece. "I have tried," he says, "both in the original Spanish and in English to like it, and I always fail. It seems to me wanting in true humour to jeer at the actions of the half-witted. It always arouses pity in me. Perhaps it is because I am a doctor and see so much mental aberration, that I cannot find pleasure in reading about such a painful subject. I think I would rather be hanged as a criminal than die semi-insane."

Don Quixote, by the way, did not die

PENCILLINGS

semi-insane. He died in his right mind, as the peaceful citizen Alonso Quixano, having made a will which disinherited his niece if she should be foolish enough to marry a man whose reading was on romances of chivalry. But that is beside the point. I have to confess myself nonplussed by the doctor's letter. I do not know how to reply to it; how to reply to it, that is, in a way which will carry conviction to him. I could say, I suppose, that Don Quixote's madness is not pathological but symbolical, that it represents the inveterate tendency of the human mind towards an idealisation of reality, and that although Cervantes gave this impulse an exaggerated embodiment, succeeding generations of men have discovered enough of the Quixote in themselves to make them feel that the story of the

FACT AND FICTION

knight's discomfiture has a universal human validity.

But argument of this kind would not convince my correspondent. It demands, in order to be convincing, a certain abstraction of the thing signified from the thing depicted, which is more difficult for some people to make than others. And, in the case of *Don Quixote,* it is, we can well believe, most difficult for a doctor. To one who is accustomed to deal with cases of actual mental aberration the realistic truth of Don Quixote's affliction must be more cogent than its inward meaning. He has seen too many Don Quixotes in real life; he has been too deeply impressed by the reality of their sufferings for it to be possible for him to regard them merely as a poetic symbol of a trick of the human soul. They touch him too nearly. Instead of reading about Don Quixote's actions as though they were imaginary events in some kingdom of the mind's potentiality, at every turn he is reminded of the doings of actual men whom he remembers, and to whom he has tried, perhaps in vain, to bring relief. In the language of Croce's philosophy, it is impossible for him to have other than a practical attitude towards Cervantes' masterpiece; the æsthetic approach is barred to him.

Although I was at first bewildered by the doctor's letter, and imagined that I was confronted with a case of literary insensibility—we all have blind spots in our faculty of literary appreciation—it seemed on further thought that his attitude, so far from being peculiar, was typical of a general

FACT AND FICTION

limitation. It is, for instance, extremely difficult for those who have been in close contact with an illness and have passed through the sickening alternation of hope and fear for lives which are dear to them, to hold themselves detached when they read an account of a like illness in fiction. Either they miss the agonising note of reality in the description and feel that the author is trifling with terrible things, or they recognise the note of reality and instinctively compare his experience with their own. A crowd of painful associations swarms up to confirm or confute the author's veracity. His book is not permitted to make its own impression, and he is judged, not as he should be, by the experience he creates in us, but by his fidelity to an experience which we recall.

PENCILLINGS

This distortion of judgment, in various forms, is continual. The simple fact that an experience has been crucial in our lives makes it peculiarly hard for us to adopt any but a practical attitude to an artistic representation of a similar experience. Men who have fought in the war are often dissatisfied with *War and Peace*. It may have been all very well when it was written, they are willing to admit, but it is not really like war. And lately I heard a young officer, who has since become a man of letters, criticise Mr. D. H. Lawrence's beautiful novel, *Aaron's Rod*, because no one who had been "through the hoop" could possibly talk as a captain of the Guards talks there. For him, as for the doctor, I had no reply ready. It seemed almost indecent to suggest that having been

FACT AND FICTION

"through the hoop" was rather a disqualification than a title to judge the book. But so it was. If we begin to test the elements of a work of literature by our own practical experience, we are on the wrong road, we are considering it not as art, but as science; not as the communication of an apprehension of life, but as a more or less faithful record of observed fact.

It is, moreover, the confusion between these two attitudes which is most frequently the cause of the strange popularity of worthless books. In *New Grub Street* Gissing declared that the royal road to success for a novelist was to deal with the very rich upper middle-class. It is, of course, only one of the roads, but it has in fact proved uncommonly successful since Gissing's time. The moderately well-to-do like to read about a condition of life which they may conceivably attain, just as elderly spinsters made the fortune of a lady-novelist who, herself an elderly spinster, invariably represented one of their kind as the beloved of an ardent, Apolline youth. The writer who can supply an imaginary satisfaction for the practical desires of a large class of people is fairly certain of financial success among that majority of readers who do not dream that the condition of entering the world of literature is to leave all practical desires behind them.

Not that the doctor and they are really comparable. It is to his honour that he cannot read of Don Quixote's adventures without pain. It proves that he has the sensitive sympathy which is necessary to his craft. A man of pure science (which a

FACT AND FICTION

doctor is not) might be far less disturbed. But those who ask for practical satisfactions from literature and find a book unreadable unless it has a happy ending deserve no such praise. Although we cannot blame them for desiring the happiness which we all desire, we can pity them for not knowing that the delight aroused by literary beauty is of a finer and more enduring kind than the fictitious realisation of their daily hopes can ever give.

WHY DO POETS WRITE?

An American professor, who has lately been trying to determine the peculiar characteristics of the poetic mind, incidentally touches upon the question: Why do poets write poetry? What is their motive in putting pen to paper? And he finds the answer in Bacon's noble sentence from the *Advancement of Learning*—one of the few scattered utterances which, were Shakespeare's works without an author, might make it conceivable that Bacon wrote them. " The use of poetry hath been to give some shadow of satisfaction to the mind of man in those points wherein the

WHY DO POETS WRITE?

nature of things doth deny it." Poetry, on this lofty theory, is written by the poet to relieve his divine discontent with the things that are and to rejoice his mind with a vision and embodiment of the things that might be.

To cast the eye of suspicion upon so high an argument seems ungenerous, if not actually cynical. Besides, it is not altogether necessary. If we do not interpret Bacon's sentence wholly in the transcendental sense which it apparently invites, we can find much poetry of which it holds good. Shelley was made for it, of course; Wordsworth fits it well with his—

" Blank misgivings of a creature
  Moving about in worlds not realised;"

So, in our own day, does Mr. De la Mare,

dreaming of the shadowless asphodel of the kingdom where neither moth nor mortality doth corrupt. But even poets less averse than these to accepting their fate as *terræ filii* reveal in their songs a longing for the things that are not. "Vivamus mea Lesbia atque amemus" is perhaps a poem of triumphant love, and it may be only our knowledge of the intolerable sequel which makes us read it as a pathetic prayer for security in a passion where no security is. But we do read it so. Love poets are seldom the singers of happiness in love, and of them certainly it is generally true that they seek for "some shadow of satisfaction to the mind in those points wherein the nature of things doth deny it."

We may, therefore, say with some reason that the characteristic emotion of poetry is

WHY DO POETS WRITE?

a longing for the things that are not, for permanence amid change, security in unrest—this " evermore unrest," as Shakespeare called it—eternity in mortality. "Bright star, would I were steadfast as thou art!" is the dominant, though sometimes scarcely audible, theme of poetry. It is "the desire of the moth for the star," no matter whether the star be given a local habitation and a name in the person of a mistress, or lifted up into the unattainable heaven as some eternal and unchanging principle of things. The poetry of acceptance, of delight without regret or triumph, without bitterness, is rare; and even in the poets who have given us a glimpse of it, it seems most often to be no more than an episode in a lifelong regret for the impossible, like a gay melody in a sombre symphony—a gaiety that seems unspeakably forlorn to our premonition of what is to come.

Nevertheless, the final effect of this emotional tone in poetry is not, as it seems it should be, discouraging. The saddest beauty is enchanting, and even if the sadness is not in the poet's mind or language, we are there to read the serenest perfection in a context of longing and disillusion. Our own delight in high poetry is symbolised by Keats's figure of "Joy whose hand is ever at his lips, Bidding adieu"; and he stands by the margin of the glorious page to warn us that there, where we have been, we cannot live. And so, if the poet is not himself sad with impossibility, we are. There is no escape. Either by expression of our own imperfect state, or by holding serenity before our eyes, he touches us to

WHY DO POETS WRITE?

tears. In this respect humanity is incorrigible. Has it not, for two thousand years, insisted on reading into Virgil's " Sunt lacrimæ rerum " a meaning which the words never had?

And yet—again we say it—the sadness inseparable from high poetry is not discouraging. It is exhilarating rather. If the poet has put it there, we are grateful to him for thinking so highly of the human soul that he regards perfection and serenity and permanence as its due. He speaks nobly, like Malvolio in the dungeon, and we thrill to his claims on our behalf; though disinherited and unrecognised, we are the sons of kings by virtue of our souls. If on the other hand it is we who supply the context of sadness to the poet's unhappiness, why then it is we ourselves who vindicate our right not to be banished from Elysium back to the world of everyday. We deserve to live with the perfections we enjoy. That we recognise them is our title to have them secured to us. Though we go barefoot we are of the blood royal. Such secret knowledge is a good viaticum.

In a sense, therefore, we are all incorrigible poets. If the poet himself had no thought of saying, "Quis desiderio sit pudor aut modus?" we say it for him. But precisely because we are in this sense all poets, precisely because we all, according to our ability, "submit the shows of things to the desires of the mind," we cannot suppose, with the American professor, that the divine discontent which we all share is the effective cause of poetry. If it were so, we should all be poets, not in a sense, but in

WHY DO POETS WRITE?

reality; that is to say, we should all be writing beautiful poems. For, after all, a real poet is a person who makes something, and though we may gladly admit that Bacon has defined what he makes better than the measurers of syllables, we cannot allow that he has revealed the reason why the poet makes it. Perhaps we might as well ask why babies are born. Perhaps, too, the answer is roughly the same to both questions, and poems, like babies, are bye-products of an activity that is self-sufficient and delightful.

STEPHEN PHILLIPS

Mr. Clutton Brock's recent reference to the case of Stephen Phillips brought two things to my mind. One was an idle discussion of badness in poetry which had ended in the safe and sound conclusion that the worst, like the finest, effects were wrung out of blank verse. (Who was it, by the way, who when asked for a definition of blank verse, defined it as the comparative of " damn bad "?) There began the usual rivalry in producing bad lines of blank verse for the general derision. " A Mr. Wilkinson, a clergyman," was, of course, exhibited. That is not a very bad line,

STEPHEN PHILLIPS

really. It is hopelessly prosaic, no doubt, but badness in poetry is a positive quality: it is not the absence of something that ought to be, but the presence of something that ought not to be there. Bad poetry is not so much prosaic as hyperpoetical. The lines we remembered were, like Wordsworth's, neutral rather than bad, and we were dissatisfied with them. Suddenly a silent member of the company said that the worst line of blank verse he had ever read was—

" The mystic yearning of a garden wet."

It was, he said, by Stephen Phillips. The competition was ended.

The other association suggested by the name of Stephen Phillips is kinder to his memory. It is an incident which, it seems

PENCILLINGS

to me, has a significance of its own. One Sunday morning in the early autumn two years ago I was walking in Hampstead, and I passed a group of people arguing in the open road in front of Jack Straw's Castle. Instinctively I slowed down to listen. As usual, they were arguing for and against Socialism. Thinking that nothing would come of it, I began to move away when my ear was caught by the name of Stephen Phillips. Instantly I was curious. What could his name be doing in that argument? I pushed my way forward and saw that a fat man of about sixty was the dominant personality. He had puffy red cheeks and small, twinkling gray eyes which continually swerved away from a hot-tempered and rather dirty young man in spectacles, with whom he was arguing,

STEPHEN PHILLIPS

and roamed benevolently over the company. With a podgy hand he fingered a thick gold watch-chain: and he wore an old, yellow straw hat. He looked like a genial and none too prosperous publican. And I naturally concluded that he was arguing against Socialism.

But not at all. It was he who had mentioned Stephen Phillips, for he mentioned him again. He stood listening with a far-away look and a patient smile to the fiery young man, who was obviously an extremist. He looked like one, and besides he violently denounced Mr. J. H. Thomas for "ratting." When he had done, the fat man said, "I don't know anything about that. What I do know is that there was a man called Stephen Phillips. He was one of the finest poets in our time, and we let him die in

PENCILLINGS

the gutter." He said it quietly, without emphasis. Nobody seemed to care. The sense of the meeting seemed to be that poets were queer fishes anyhow, and you couldn't afford to worry about what happened to them.

The fat man was a little disgusted. "Perhaps you've never heard of Stephen Phillips?" he said to us all. There was no answer. "Well," he sighed, "he was a fine poet, he was, and he finished up by having to cadge for a shilling for a drink. *We* let him die." He paused. "I don't know anything about this young gentleman's ideas," he went on. "I'm old-fashioned," he said, with a charming smile. "I've worked hard, and I've read a few books, and I don't want my books or my little house taken away. But I do say

STEPHEN PHILLIPS

there's something b—— wrong with a country that lets a poet like Stephen Phillips die in the gutter. That's the kind of thing that makes me a Socialist." He spoke so quietly that every one was impressed and silent, except the young man with the spectacles.

"Have you read Karl Marx's *Capital*?" he asked the fat man truculently.

"As much as I could, I have, young man. A red-covered book. I got it at home."

"Well?" said the young man very meaningly.

"Well," said the fat man, smilingly, "I don't like it 'alf so much as *John Ball's Dream*."

I do not know whether the fat man's account of Stephen Phillips's end is true, though he spoke as one who had known him in his latter days, and perhaps had given him the shillings. But it seems to me that Stephen Phillips's memory gains rather than loses by the story. It is no small thing for a poet to have been regarded with such kindly reverence by an honest man, and to have become for him the symbol of genius and the misfortunes of genius. That achievement should weigh heavily in the scales against the bad lines he perpetrated. For me at any rate his memory is indissolubly united with that of his generous champion. For him I have a peculiar affection. Perhaps he was ineffectual: perhaps it is the mark of the Socialist dreamer to prefer *The Dream of John Ball* to *Das Kapital*: but the quality of the preference is somehow pleasant. And at

STEPHEN PHILLIPS

any rate he was one of those unselfish souls to whom—

> " the miseries of the world
> Are misery, and will not let them rest,"

They are the salt of the earth.

BEAUTY-HUNTING

In a foreword to a catalogue of an exhibition of paintings by Sir John and Lady Lavery, Mr. Winston Churchill wrote these words concerning the pictures of the lady.

"If I were a Master of Hounds hunting Beauty, I should have no hesitation, at the end of the run, in handing her the Brush."

It is one of those striking sentences dropped from the heights which we poor mortals, who neither are, nor are likely to be, Privy Councillors, carry about in our heads for days. We have been haunted by it; we have dreamed dreams. It fits so well with our conception of the right honourable

BEAUTY-HUNTING

gentleman who uttered it. It is in itself a gesture, a vision. The red-coated M.F.H. gallops up, sweeps off his velvet cap. We see him on the sky-line for a moment, turn our jaded horses home and talk in jerks about the run.

A vision! More than one. For if each man in his life plays many parts, Mr. Winston Churchill in his has played the parts of many men. Instead of a nice, simple M.F.H. galloping up, he begins to expand, to duplicate himself. He becomes like one of those multi-musical Italian wanderers, with a big drum on their shoulders, an accordion in their hands, a chime of bells on their hats, and a triangle in their teeth. So Mr. Churchill appears with an easel on his back, a polo-stick lightly held in place of a hunting-crop, hallooing, in place of the too familiar " Gone away, away," the simple little ditty set for him by Max Beerbohm:—

> " We want eight,
> And we won't wait! "

It is no wonder a man so many-sided should juggle with his metaphors. It is his privilege. And how breezy and downright it is, to be sure! The manifest utterance of a man with no nonsense about him! But not a simple man. No! A man who can beat the literary gentlemen at their own game. And, to tell the truth, he nearly did once, with his *River War*. Who of the mere professional writers would have attempted a pun and a metaphor at the same time? Mr. Churchill's incorrigible versatility will not be denied even in a sentence.

BEAUTY-HUNTING

We feel it is a characteristic sentence, and at the same time that we have not yet touched on the real reason why it seems so characteristic. We must apply the methods of advanced criticism to it. Here we have a passage in which, we feel, our author's sensibility is completely expressed. We have already disentangled one strand from it—an incorrigible versatility. Lurking behind the sentence we discern the Winston of Mr. Low's unkind cartoons, dressed in an admiral's hat and cavalry boots. But there is something more than this. After all, why shouldn't a man be versatile? Why shouldn't he kill two birds with one stone if he can?

There is no reason at all, provided that both birds needed killing. The unnecessary killing of birds, in real life and in metaphors,

PENCILLINGS

is deplorable. Mr. Churchill wants to pay Lady Lavery a compliment on her painting. If he were a Master of Hounds hunting Beauty, he says gallantly, he would have no hesitation in handing her the Brush at the end of the run. The lady blushes and bows; then she thinks it over. She has plenty of time to think over it, for the remark is in print and in its third edition by now. First she discovers that it is not she but Mr. Churchill who leads the pursuit of Beauty. He is the general of the campaign, she a distinguished assistant. It is not quite so gallant as it seemed. But then she remembers that Mr. Churchill himself has toiled with canvas and tubes. There is such a thing as seniority. Mr. Churchill was painting years ago; he took to the craft in one of the brief intervals in which

BEAUTY-HUNTING

he was spared the task of directing operations on the Western Front. It would have been a *beau geste* in him to have forgotten it; but a mind conscious of mastery has a right to insist on its own pre-eminence. Courtesy must sometimes bow to truth. And we remember that it was a great thing to be granted a tabouret in the full rays of the Roi Soleil.

Lady Lavery may perhaps feel that the compliment was a shade too nicely adjusted to their respective eminences in the art of beauty-hunting. A little more generosity and a little less etiquette would have made the praise still sweeter. But she has nothing to complain of. The Master would have given her the brush; and he has put it on record.

But what has happened to poor Beauty?

PENCILLINGS

We have forgotten all about her. Alas! she has been butchered to make a *bon mot*. Lady Lavery has the brush, to be sure; but the hounds have the rest. Beauty has gone to the dogs. A few bits of bloody fur—and the brush—are all that remains of her. Perhaps, as she carries away her trophy, Lady Lavery's eyes may catch sight of the raw and bleeding stump, and she may wonder whether she has been paid a compliment at all.

Many minds of many men have pursued Beauty through all the ages with thought and imagination, in joy and despair. They have followed her in ecstasy and agony, in triumph and torment; but the agonies and torments have been their own. They have seen her dimly with Truth at her side; they have gone in quest of her with adora-

BEAUTY-HUNTING

tion and a trembling fear of their own unworthiness to touch the hem of her garment. If any were cruel, it was she and not they. Keats and Baudelaire, who spent lives of suffering on the quest, declared that she was implacable, motionless, sovereign. "Jamais je ne pleure," she said to Baudelaire, "et jamais je ne ris." But they did not hate her for it. They only loved her the more; they approached her with a deeper reverence, a more heartfelt fear. And, since Plato first discerned her, enthroned apart, high above the flux of imperfect things, the mind of civilisation has moved towards her in this mood.

It has been left to the Rt. Hon. Winston Spencer Churchill, P.C., M.P., to set it right. He was the first man to see that

PENCILLINGS

there is no point in all this palaver. If you want to catch a rat, take a dog to him. If you want to catch Beauty, take a dog to her. O, you infatuated poets, priests and philosophers who have wasted more than two thousand years in paying your stammering suits to the lady of your desire, could you not see that her long delay was due to your own timidity? She would have yielded long ago had not the great minds of the world been busy with greater things—deciding what fur a bearskin should be made of, and teaching the Prince of Wales to play polo. But at last a man has arisen who can dispose of these affairs of State so swiftly that he has time to spare for the things of the spirit. He takes a quick, Napoleonic glance at the new world to conquer. He looks along the ages and

BEAUTY-HUNTING

sees generations of men timidly advancing towards the veiled goddess. Fools! What can Beauty do against his beauties? "Have at her!"

Now for the first time a view-hulloa echoes through the fields of Art. A splendid run, without a single check, for poor Beauty has not learned the rudiments of the noble game. A kill in the open!

But who are these dishevelled, breathless followers on foot? Why do they wave their arms and wring their hands? What are they shouting for, and why are they wildly gesticulating? "What have you done?" comes the faint cry in the gathering dusk. "What have I done!" roars the Master. "Why, what you've been trying to do since God knows when, you idiots. . . . What have I done! Caught Beauty for you, you fools!" "But . . . you've killed her," stammers the foremost, short and pale and blown. Johnny Keats always did have bellows to mend. "What the devil did you expect me to do with her, then?"

No, there is no answer. How could they understand each other? "There's no doing anything to help these d——d fellows," growls the Master. And, to relieve his sense of injustice received, he curses his first Whip as he rides sulkily away.

Then, in spite of himself, his mind turns back to serious things. His annoyance is slowly dissolved by cares of State. Suddenly a spark of joy gleams in his eye; he cracks his whip in his delight. Those busbies for the Guards! The very thing!

BEAUTY-HUNTING

The skin of Beauty! Original, striking, never thought of before. He begins to prepare his speech on the Army Estimates; he hears the murmur of wonder at the epoch-making innovation.

Good God! He'd forgotten. He's no longer at the War Office. Why on earth did he take the Colonies? You can't give an idea like that to a man like Worthington-Evans.

The announcement of the change in the Cabinet is expected at any moment.

ON GRAMMAR

As we get older, most of us begin to forget that such a thing as grammar exists. We remember the name but not the thing. Occasionally in a vindictive mood—very often the result of ten minutes with that delightful but mortifying volume, *The King's English*—we pounce upon some one else's grammar and declare it is all wrong. For the rest, grammar is a vague memory of Latin gender rhymes—

" as *curculio, vespertilio,*
pugio, scipio, and *papilio*—"

of syntax tags (which seem to the sceptical

ON GRAMMAR

eye of manhood only a choice collection of the ungrammatical practices of the ancients), and of that tremendous process called "parsing." I remember being asked at a very tender age to "parse" two lines which surely came from *The Lady of the Lake*—

"So swift of foot, his eagle eye
The ptarmigan in snow could spy...."

Some one will tell me I have misquoted it. Scott never wrote such bad sense. Shakespeare did, anyhow. And it was my examiner who quoted it, and not I.

But the point is, it did not worry me in the least that swift runners should necessarily be long-sighted. I was perfectly prepared to accept that. The real brick—slang, I

PENCILLINGS

fear—but still . . . the real brick was the ptarmigan. The only other "pt" I had ever heard of (and Heaven alone knows how I had heard of that) was "pterodactyl." A "pterodactyl" was a fossil. A fossil could not possibly have "spied" the gentleman's eye, even if it was an eagle. Therefore, the gentleman spied the fossil. "*Ptarmigan:* noun, concrete, object of verb 'spy.'" You, who have forgotten your grammar, do not know that that is the correct answer. I scored ten out of ten.

But that "ptarmigan" haunted me for many years afterwards. It made two critical reappearances. About two years later I happened to be taken to the real London, and I saw on the outside of a discreet West-End poulterer's—how unlike what a

ON GRAMMAR

poulterer's should be!—the legend "Dealers in Black Game and Ptarmigan." I immediately conceived a great contempt for the hero of the unforgotten lines. A ptarmigan was a bird, and he was black. Why, I could see a black bird in snow myself! Yards away. And then I began to brood over the lines again, and it occurred to me that it was the black bird that did the spying after all. But then there was the problem of my full marks. It was too difficult. Either the poet was a fool, or my examiner a knave. I let the matter rest.

The next avatar of that ghostly fowl was when I began Greek. There are quite a number of "pt's" in Greek. The first one for which I conceived any real affection was "ptuo." It seemed to me then, and it seems to me now, a much more eloquent word than "spit," and—in another relation—a much better word than "tupto." "Tupto" was altogether too ladylike. It bore about the same relation to its meaning as "punish" does to "beat." In fact, a silly word. But the most definite result of these early explorations of the Greek tongue was the discovery that "pt" was quite an ordinary occurrence. "Ptarmigan" became a Greek word. By the time I had a Liddell and Scott of my own, I had forgotten the problem. So to this day "ptarmigan" has remained vaguely Greek. Something tells me it is probably Gaelic; but something else that it ought to be Greek, as it ought to be black. "Melas, melaina, melan; Ptarmigas, ptarmigaina, ptarmigan."

ON GRAMMAR

The consequence (to which these confessions are the preliminary) is that grammar to me is irrevocably mixed up with "ptarmigan." One might almost say that it *is* ptarmigan. From ptarmigan to caviare is the shortest of steps; hardly a step at all in that distinguished poulterer's shop—a matter of reaching from a hook to a shelf. I wonder to how many little boys grammar is at this moment in process of a similar mysterious change. After all, these incorporeal, transcendental entities have to be brought to earth somehow. "The soul of our grandam might haply inhabit a bird." Mine was only a more traditional metempsychosis than is usually the case. Some Egyptian atavism guided my choice, and my maturer philosophy approves. In this matter I feel rather like the slave of

PENCILLINGS

Meno who was born with the knowledge that the square of the hypotenuse is equal to the sum of the squares of the other two sides.

But I should dearly love to ask other little boys, with sad and studious faces, "What is grammar?"; to ask my question in a tone quite different from that of the examiner, to make it a matter of confidence, a secret between ourselves. For little boys have not—thank heaven—learned the detestable habit of abandoning their souls to a block of paper. Probably I should have to lead the way. I would observe quite casually: "I think it's a kind of bird." If I said ptarmigan it would sound like a secret society. It would be too exciting, and produce bad dreams. I wonder what he would reply. The pessimism that is the

ON GRAMMAR

Sancho Panza to my romanticism whispers unkindly: "The science of language." Good Lord!

An admirable little book—in truth the only begetter of these meanderings—comes, like a fresh breeze, to disperse the cloud of foreboding. Dr. Philip Ballard convinces me that the little boy would reply with an incredulous stare. "Grammar! Never heard of it!" That is almost rude, of course. But I have imagination, and I can see from Dr. Ballard's book that young Ernest will not be sad and studious at all. Far from it! He will be accustomed to deliver concise orations on the burning topics of the hour —Labour and Capital, for instance, to quote my authority—to an audience infinitely more critical than I should ever be. Why should he stand on ceremony with me?

PENCILLINGS

He will have the habit of discussing the merits of Nick Carter as compared to those of Sexton Blake with a master who is a connoisseur of this kind of literature, and who—wisely, but yet how boldly!—insists that little boys get vastly more good (yes, *good*) out of something they do read than something they don't. I shall be able to discuss the style, technical and literary, of Nelson Lee with him; but an answer to my question: "What is grammar?" I may not hope to receive.

For grammar nowadays is not a ptarmigan, nor a railway train, nor the man in the moon; it is merely dead. That is, in a way, less exciting; but it is much less dangerous. Romanticist though I am, I cannot believe that my pursuit of elusive entity in the semblance of a fowl did me very much

ON GRAMMAR

good. More good than "the science of language," no doubt, for that was only a sudden impediment in speech, which made me choke and turn red as a turkey-cock. "He was running out of Hall with Biggy Jones and me . . . Biggy Jones and I, sir." Now, young Ernest says unblushingly: "Biggy Jones and me." Instead of that curious sense of living in two worlds, in one of which he speaks like a rational human being, while in the other he talks pure Sandford and Merton, or would do if he could only get the hang of it, he lives in a world full of heroes, beginning with himself, rising by gradual stages through Nick Carter to the Count of Monte Cristo and Rupert of Hentzau, through Jim Hawkins to the last perfection of an Antony and a Brutus—the noblest Roman of them all.

PENCILLINGS

But all are noble Romans, and all speak (with their proper variations) the right Roman language, that is an English that can be understood from one man to another.

Of course that is not exactly a real world. But what small boy ever desired to live in a real world? What has taken the place of the problem of grammar is the problem of making the boy enter this more than real world of literature and keeping him there, keeping him there long enough to make him forget the uncouth pidgin-English of the London streets or the insipid slang—the " niceness " and the " jolliness "—of the middle-class home. Dr. Ballard is optimistic, but I gather that not even he regards the new problem as solved. Part of the solution rests, no doubt, with the authors. They must set themselves, as Stevenson did, to

ON GRAMMAR

write adventure stories which will make Nick Carter and Nelson Lee pale their ineffectual fires. But, if they do, will their stories ever find their way into the class-room? Is *Treasure Island* even now a prescribed, or even a permitted, text in the elementary schools? As far as I know the only modern literature that finds its way into an educational syllabus is anthologies of modern poetry. The *Lady of the Lake* was better than that.

If Dr. Ballard himself had the ordering of these things we could be fairly confident that a solution would be found, even without the active co-operation of the authors. Dr. Ballard knows how to write, and he obviously knows a good story when he sees one. (And this although he presumes to say that the words of a little girl of four had " outstripped her ideas " because she declared that " all

PENCILLINGS

the little butterflies and burglars have gone to bed." Even I could construct a whole universe on so firm a foundation.) What would happen if Dr. Ballard had the ordering of these things is that the author of a really good story, who had long since despaired of being read by that suburban society that is impassioned only by the passions of Mayfair, would wake up one morning and discover that he had been run over-night into ten editions by special request of the L.C.C.

Yet, even so, a problem would remain. Suppose that young Ernest comes—as at least half the young Ernests do come—from some noisome Backwater Alley. Suppose that, under Dr. Ballard's beneficent *régime,* he reads much and is thrilled by what he reads, so that he understands the speech of this magnificent world where

ON GRAMMAR

you make as little fuss of running away with a well-found pearl schooner as he does in actual life of running away with a bad orange from under a hawker's barrow. Will he ever be induced to refer to his own exploit in the language which belongs to the other? Will he ever learn to say, "I made good my escape," instead of "I done a bunk"? He might conceivably say it to the police magistrate, but not to the policeman, and far less to the boon companion to whom alone he can describe his achievement with the full ardor of conviction. He will still learn his language from the streets where he lives, the music-hall songs he hears, and the public-houses that Colonel Gretton and Mr. Bottomley would like to see him freely entering again. Still, by Dr. Ballard's method one small boy in a

PENCILLINGS

dozen will be brought into the right way, where grammar has never saved a single brand from the burning. And for the eleven others? "Let me build your streets, let me make your public-houses and your songs, and I will make your sons speak English." It is the old argument; perhaps it will be the old reply: "If you make my streets, my public-houses and my songs, I will neither live nor drink in them; neither will I let young Ernie sing them."

S. P. E.

Now that it has issued its fourth tract, the Society for Pure English seems, in these days of brief literary lives, to have become an institution. I begin to feel that these little books, filled with charming admonitions and horrid warnings, will never cease their patient visitations until I am *emeritus* and have hung the wooden pen upon my walls. Their sedate habiliment of buff, their decorous typography, their discreet approach, their soft tapping at the door of the literary conscience, remind me of some early Quaker gently admonishing a brother for backsliding. Without a doubt, " Brother " is the address they use; and

PENCILLINGS

the latest of them has recalled to me a vivid and tremendous vision of my school days.

The school where I learned my declensions was reverend and glorious, and the masters who taught them were reverend and glorious too. One of these heroic figures had a heroic temper. C's wrath was as the wrath of Achilles, and like Achilles he would sulk within his tent. But the doors of his tent were always open, for the partition which divided the terrors of his class-room from the calm of ours was of glass. Through this we would watch the miserable boy, who had (in Greek) made a masculine crocodile lay eggs, tremble before C's thundered indignation, reverberating through the dim grammar-school. Our own kindly usher would take off his benevo-lent spectacles, blush red as a child, and

S. P. E.

march with quick little steps up and down, murmuring "Terrible, terrible," and quivering with restrained remonstrances. Our lesson stopped dead, while the great passionate voice roared on. A superstitious dread fell upon us as we peered silently into the other room, waiting for the inevitable apparition.

Truly, I believe our hearts missed a beat when we saw C's door slowly begin to open. *Incessu patuit deus.* C's voice dropped into silence like a stone. Our usher's marching suddenly ceased, and he stared blushing at the ground. And then we heard the still, small voice: "*Brother* C——; *Brother* C——." The door closed as delicately as it had opened.

That was all. I must have watched the fearful epiphany a dozen times. The Head was a dark man, neat and small and rotund. Yet I never heard him say to C., whom memory makes a giant, more than the one phrase, "*Brother* C——; *Brother* C——." Nor was there a hint of threatening in his reticence. He know the nature as he knew the periods of C's wrath; therefore he knew it was enough to tap lightly at the door of his conscience.

Such is the appearance—neat, decorous, small, discreet—of an S. P. E. tract, and such its effect upon me. "Brother M——," sounds the voice; and I look into my soul for my sins. Do I pronounce *metal* the same as *mettle*? Heavens above, I can detect no difference. *Mettle* . . . *mettle* . . . *met-tall* . . . *met-tal*? Then with a deep-drawn breath of relief, I see that I am not damned for that. "A careful English

S. P. E.

speaker "—what would I not give to be that man?—find that " he does not *naturally* distinguish between *mettle* and *metal* in pronunciation." Blessings upon him! I admire him. I will follow the simple courage of his resolution, with its almost human caution. " So I intend in future to pronounce *metal* as *metal* (when I don't forget)." And so, by the grace of God, do I—if only I knew what *metal* sounded like. But I will find out, I will find out.

But the Careful English Speaker is bound to wring my withers soon. " When I hear *principal* pronounced as *principle* it gives me a squirm, though I am afraid nearly everybody does it now." To be one of the indistinguishable mass—what a prick to my vanity! *Principle* . . . *principal* . . . *pul* . . . *pal* . . . Was it a dream? Or did

PENCILLINGS

I really hear some infinitesimal nuance that redeems me from the vulgar herd? Or was it only the deceitful echo of my extreme desire? The thought that I should have lived to make the Careful English Speaker squirm is gall and vitriol to me. Perhaps my nuance of a nuance will save me: perhaps when he hears me speak, when I walk along the chalk line saying clearly, seven times in succession: "The principal thing is that our pronunciation should not be ruled by principle," I shall not cause him a squirm, or even a wince—nothing worse than the lift of an eyebrow.

But if my gentle remonstrant in buff (or is it snuff?) humiliates me sometimes, at others he exalts my self-esteem. I feel immeasurably superior to those of my fellow-journalists who risk the word

S. P. E.

"protagonist" and use it wrong. Indeed, I was already feeling fairly comfortable in my mind about *protagonist* and my eye was complacently skimming a page-full of illegitimate uses culled from the writings of my less fortunate colleagues, when suddenly I saw. . . .

It was a singular piece of good fortune; perhaps not entirely deserved. I am not naturally conceited, and when an S. P. E. tract and I have been reasoning together a little while, I am more than ordinarily humble. It was not, therefore, any impulse of pride that led me at first to skip the "legitimate uses" of *protagonist* and pass to the study of the "absurd uses." I was, half-consciously, anxious to be reassured. To be honest, I was reassured. My confidence came back to me. So confident

PENCILLINGS

indeed did I become that I began to join in the scholarly chuckle at the vainglorious and foolhardy man—was ever a purer case of *hubris*?—who wrote: "The protagonists in the drama, which has the motion and structure of a Greek tragedy. . . ." In short, I was feeling at my ease, perhaps even a little hubristical myself. I turned back to the "legitimate uses" without a tremor of misgiving. At a glance I saw that there were only two examples—rare, rare is the journalist who knows this gambit! This is, indeed, the shibboleth of shibboleths, thought I. And then. . . .

It dawned upon me slowly, as slowly as it will dawn upon me when I read my own name in capitals at the top of the Honours List, created Baron for my services to literature. Not quicker than this and with

S. P. E.

no smaller thrill of incredulous astonishment, did it dawn upon me that I—yes, I—was the author of the first passage—*inter pares,* perhaps, but indisputably *primus*—in which the *protagonist* trick was correctly performed! There was I, elevated to the bench, sitting next to, conversing quietly with, the Careful Speaker of English. I cannot quote the sentence. Readers of my collected works would recognise it, and me. This essay would then become conceited. But there it is, enthroned on the top of page 41. It is really worth it, to spend a half-crown on S. P. E. Tract No. IV. for that alone; for it is a singularly pretty piece of work. I myself have spent several hours admiring it.

And if this alone should seem an insufficient return for a half-crown, consider

PENCILLINGS

these further arguments. There is one other sentence unclaimed. It may be yours, dear reader. Of course, you cannot hope to be *primus,* but you may be indisputably *par.* On the other hand, there are risks: fourteen "absurd uses." You may draw one of them. Still, you can keep it to yourself, and you will have learned your lesson. Secondly, consider that, even though you receive neither canonisation nor excommunication in this matter of *protagonist,* half an hour in the confessional with the little man in buff, or snuff, will have a tonic effect upon your literary conscience. If it slumbers, he will awake it; if it is drowsy, he will make it alert; if it is awake, he will spur it into activity. Mine is, I admit, not an ordinary case. He has made me bold, not to say thrasonical. I

S. P. E.

am become a hot-gospeller, a crusader. Dr. Henry Bradley himself is timid and lukewarm compared to me. He points out that we have now no proper word for a member of the healing profession. Doctor, you say? Doctor should be the privileged title of those who have taken their doctor's degree. Doctor Johnson, I am sure, would not have tolerated a Bachelor of Medicine who usurped the name of Doctor. Dr. Bradley reminds us that there is a word, a good word—" leech." But at the thought of trying to revive it, his courage fails. " If I were to introduce my medical attendant to a friend with the words, ' This is my leech ' . . . he would not consider the joke to be in the best of taste." In my present mood, these politic thoughts are cowardly. I *will* call my doctor a leech.

PENCILLINGS

But these heights of resolution are not for ordinary men. They must content themselves, when next their leech humiliates them by prodding them familiarly with his stethoscope, with thinking what they might call him if only they had my good fortune and my courage. But on a lower level they will be vastly benefited by a course of S. P. E. It will give them a feeling of awareness when they speak and when they write which will, if they persevere, develop into a feeling of virtuosoship. They will pass far beyond the stage of being unable to confuse " feasible " with " possible "; they will be on the *qui vive* for an opportunity to give a good old word a new lease of life and the death-blow to a bad new one. They will be promoted to the proud rank of Guardians of the Republic of Speech and

S. P. E.

Letters. And they can be this, or they can fulfil an essential condition of being this, by sending half a guinea to the Secretary of the S. P. E., 11 St. Leonard's Terrace, Chelsea. In return they will receive four tracts, whose potency they may judge by the effect that one alone has had upon me.